Reuniting the People of God

Edited by

Dr. A. Charles Ware, president
Baptist Bible College of Indianapolis

Eugene Seals, president
Quality Publishing Systems

A Quality Book™

Reuniting the People of God
Second in the Multicultural Ministry Series

Edited by Dr. A. Charles Ware and Eugene Seals

Published by:

Baptist Bible College of Indianapolis
601 North Shortridge Road
Indianapolis, IN 46219
317-352-8736

Unless otherwise indicated, Scripture quotations are from the King James Version.

(The first book in the Multicultural Ministry Series by Dr. A. Charles Ware, *Prejudice and the People of God*, is available through the publisher.)

Printed in the United States of America.

A very special thanks

to all those who recognize the Biblical imperative to
reconcile humans to each other and to God.

— Dr. A. Charles Ware

Contents

Reflections

The 1998 Multiracial Reconciliation Conference provided outstanding challenges from the Word of God. The powerful models presented inspired us to strive with integrity toward greater faithfulness in the area of race relations. I continue to thank God for the privilege of being associated with an institution with such a vision.

Baptist Bible College of Indianapolis (BBCI) was begun in 1980 by the late Dr. James Wells (an African American pastor), Dr. Clint Kaulfield, and Rev. Ken Davis (two white gentlemen). Many people have served over the years, and I have been privileged to participate in this ministry. I am excited that we have been putting on the biennial Multiracial Reconciliation Conferences. At BBCI, we try to model racial reconciliation. We have an integrated board, an integrated staff, and an integrated student body.

As I champion racial reconciliation around then country, I talk about the responsibilities of all people. Frankly, the way I live right now, I do not see color as a defining characteristic of human beings. I see my staff as individuals with character. I do not think consciously about color because I am immersed in God and doing His work. Contrary to the pattern in vogue in our land, I want BBCI to reflect what we talk about. May our God richly bless all who endeavor to live courageous lives of integrity before our Maker and our neighbors.

– A. Charles Ware

1 – Do You See What I See?

— A. Charles Ware[1]

What do you see happening in the world? In the church? Do you see what I see? Consider what the Scripture says in Matthew 5:13-16,

> You are the salt of the earth, but if the salt has lost its savor, wherewith shall it be salted? It is thenceforth good for nothing but to be cast out and to be trodden under foot of men. You are the light of the world. A city that is set on a hill cannot be hid. Neither do men light a candle and put it under a bushel, but on a candlestick, and it giveth light unto all that are in the house. Let your light so shine before men that they may see your good works and glorify your Father, which is in Heaven.

Space does not permit me to tell you about everything I see in the world. However, here are a few items on my radar screen. What I see is not racial reconciliation, but polarization. I see people arguing, fussing, and fighting with one another to get their way. This world does not give me any great hope for reconciliation.

---

[1] Dr. A. Charles Ware is president of Baptist Bible College of Indianapolis. The founder of the Voice of Biblical Reconciliation, he is a tireless advocate for multiracial ministry.

At the same time, sometimes what I see in the church is not too encouraging either. In fact, I had two people make interesting observations recently. One black fellow said,

> We went to those Promise Keepers meetings and got all excited. Then we wanted to have some men's meetings back here locally in Indianapolis that would bring blacks, whites, and other races together. We sponsored local conferences for two years. The attendance was so low, it was pathetic. I do not want to discourage you, but we gave it up. We went back to just having our men's meetings.

Another black leader in the area said,

> God must have brought you to me because some of us have tried this before, but we lost hope. I know that what you are doing is right, however, because I know it is Biblical. I just hope you can do something.

People are losing hope, even in the church. In Matthew 5:16, we are told to "Let your light so shine." I want to underscore that. We are not the *light*. He is the light. If we have been born again, He is the one who lights all men. If Christ has lighted us, let Him shine so that men may see.

We have a lot of talk but little walk. People hear our profession, but they do not see our actions. One of the most desperate things we need in this whole racial reconciliation discussion is some models — people of integrity that others can see. We run around telling people how we love one another, how we have been saved, redeemed by the blood of Christ; and how we are one big happy family. If they look at us, however, what do they see? I am sorry to say that the picture we present is scarcely better than what the world presents. People need to see our good works. Saints should show forth the Savior.

Matthew 5:13-16 also says, "...glorify your Father which is in heaven." Sinners will give praise to the Father as a result of seeing our good works. Instead of that, people often curse our Father because they see our un-Christian works. We too often blame, offend, and refuse to talk to one another in a civilized way. We do not sing or worship together. We do not do anything together.

Tragedy Bridging Racial Lines

As bleak as the picture is, sometimes there is cause for optimism. On February 26, 1998, while I was in the state of Washington, my executive vice-president called to inform me that my son, Matt, had been seriously injured in a basketball practice. I called the hospital and spoke with a nurse who told me that Matt had broken his neck and was paralyzed from the shoulders down. The nurse put my wife Sharon on the phone.

Sharon was disturbed. "Matt has been injured, and it does not look good," she said, motherly concern obvious in her voice. "But, I have to leave now; they are putting him in the ambulance to take him to another hospital." That was all the communication I received that afternoon, leaving me with a feeling of helplessness, 2500 miles from home. What I would not have given for wings of an eagle or a private plane to rush to the side of my wife and my son.

I went back to the seminary where I was preaching and advised the people that my son had been paralyzed and that I had to go home. The seminarians empathized with our situation. Someone said, "Brother, let us pray." We fell on our knees.

I prayed for two things specifically: The first was, "God, give Matt a supernatural sense of your presence. He needs to know you in a way that only you can make yourself known." Then I prayed for my wife, "God, I do not know why I am way out here in Seattle." I recalled how I had changed that speaking engagement three times. I had never changed an engagement that many times before. I began to sense that I was where God wanted me at that time.

My second request of Almighty God was, "My wife needs comfort. Please comfort her somehow."

The first flight I could get out of Seattle was at 1:00 a.m. Therefore, I went ahead and preached that night. Then I packed and we prayed again before I left for the airport. At the airport, I found myself sitting with Brother Ken Hutcherson, who later that year preached the final service at our multiracial reconciliation conference. He and his assistant had come to the airport at midnight to strengthen me and pray with me.

The words I remember most from that hour before I boarded the plane were, "Brother, we want you to know something. Do not worry. God is going to take care of everything."

I had never met them before that previous Sunday. Now, do you see what I see? You might be thinking, "Yeah. They prayed with you; and they sat with you; and they prayed with you some more." Nevertheless, there is more to it than that. The first group was white. We fell on our knees together and prayed to God for my family. The two men who came to the airport were black. I see something happening here. God's people were praying for our family! There was no angel in Heaven saying, "We are going to answer their prayers because they are the right color." Their prayers were prompted and heard because of a common bond – Jesus. I needed somebody to pray. The blood of Christ is there for all.

I see racial reconciliation as the right thing to do. I know it's right because in my first book, *Prejudice and the People of God*, I tried to lay out my perspective on this whole thing. It is right because Jesus said, "Other sheep I have which are not in this fold; them too must I bring." Jesus used Samaritan Gentiles as illustrations to show Jews that His Body was bigger than the Jewish people.

I know it's right because before Jesus went back to glory, He gave that Great Commission, "Go into ALL the world and make disciples of ALL nations." Furthermore, in Acts 1:8, Jesus said,

> But you shall receive power after the Holy Ghost has come upon you, and you shall be witnesses unto me, both in Jerusalem and Judea and in Samaria and to the uttermost parts of the earth.

Some say that Acts 1:8 defines a geographical strategy wherein you evangelize your hometown, then your neighboring towns, and then other towns. I could not disagree more. Acts 1:8 is a racial strategy. *Jerusalem* is a city where Jews lived. *Judea* was a little farther out, comparable to our county or state. *Samaritans* were half-breed Jews who lived in a ghetto despised by the "self-respecting" Jews of that day. The *Gentiles* were a completely different ethnic group.

I know it is right because when I studied the book of Acts, the disciples did what Jesus told them to do in Acts 1:8. On the Day of Pentecost, they began to preach the message to the Jews. Later, in Acts 8, the Ethiopian Eunuch got the message. Then the message went to the despised Samaritans through Philip. Finally, it went to the utmost parts of the earth, starting with Peter's preaching to the Gentiles.

In Acts 15, the Apostles convened a council where they had a chance to say that God wants separate churches, that God wants everybody conformed to one little image. Instead, they decided that Jews are saved through the same process as everyone else.

In Acts 10:28, Peter told them, "It was not lawful for me, being a Jew, to go into the house of a person of another nation." But God told Peter that God had broken down the middle wall of partition, that He has made of two, one new man. We are fellow citizens now. We have equal access. After they discussed the matter in the church, they pronounced a major New Testament doctrine. I do not understand why people do not see it.

I see God's reconciling work from my study of the book of Ephesians, where a Jew writes to the Gentiles and tells them that there was social segregation that God did not approve of.

People say, "Well but, but, but...but we have got differences. We have got cultures." 1 Corinthians 8-11 talks about cultural differences in the church. Romans 15 talks about cultural differences in the church, and

Paul still says, "With one mind and one mouth, we need to glorify God." Do you see what I see?

The Pastoral Epistles exhorted people not to get hung up on foolish genealogies. After centuries of some people claiming that Jesus was a western European, some people are now running around trying to prove that Jesus was black. I got a call from BET – Black Entertainment Television. They said, "We want you to debate Dr. Cain Hope Felder. He's saying Jesus was black. What do you have to say?"

I said, "I do not know what color He was, and I do not know what difference it makes." Some black people are trying to say that if Jesus was black, then we can feel significant. Does that mean white people are supposed to feel insignificant? The people who tried to kill Jesus were the Jews. Let me tell you something. It was not His color. It was His doctrine and character. Unless you were a Jew – in their minds, you could be black, white, or polka dot – you still were on the outside.

Even though there were black Jews, tell me, what difference does it make? Jesus asked, "Why call you me 'Lord, Lord,' and do not the things which I say?"

Those people who tried to claim some type of superiority because Jesus was of Jewish stock, boasted, "We be not sinners like those Gentiles. We be of our father Abraham."

Jesus corrected them, "You are of your father, the Devil." Do you see what I see?

Every Tribe and Nation. What brings us into the *family* of God is that we have been born by the *Spirit* of God through the death of the *Son* of God. I know it's right because I have read the end of the story. Revelation 7 describes saints from every tribe, every tongue, and every nation around the throne of God.

Some people say, "I do not want to go to a certain church because of *that kind* of people. I do not want to be with *them*."

I tell them, "You do not want to go to heaven then, do you, because *they* will be there. Furthermore, I have some more bad news for you. You had better not go to Hell either, because *they* will be there, too."

So, do you see what I see? That is why I put that in my book. It's right because it is Biblical. I am talking about reconciliation rooted in redemption by God and guided by revelation. I see a family, the family of God. I was not looking for the color. I was looking for the character of the people who were praying for my son. As I boarded that plane and took that long ride back home, I cried sometimes. I remember saying to myself, "God, you know I gave you my life. I will be anything you want me to be. However, my son is paralyzed. I will have to move to a home that will be more accessible for a paralyzed person. I do not have money to move. God, I am going to lose my job. I cannot serve you full time anymore. I am going to have to get two or three jobs because I have to take care of my son."

I remember thinking about our oldest son, Tim, who was graduating from college. I was going to have to ask him, "Come home, son. Live with your family. Get a job. Help us take care of your brother."

After struggling with God for a bit, I surrendered and said, "All right, God. Whatever *You* want." Do you see what I see? I landed in Indianapolis and went to the hospital where I began to hear the story. It seems that when my wife arrived at the hospital, she was distraught, crying, weeping for her son. As she wept, Matt, who was paralyzed, looked at her and said, "Mom, pull yourself together. Remember, God is in control."

Now, did God answer the white people's prayer or the black people's prayer to comfort my son? God answered the prayer of His people. Matt's statement was so astounding that a newspaper writer who happened to be on the scene picked it up. The next day the *Indianapolis Star* carried the following front-page headline:

Athlete Injured, But not His Spirit

A story about my son! I told him, "Matt, look at this. At 16 years of age, how good would you have to play basketball to get on the front page of the *Indianapolis Star*? Even the Indianapolis Pacers basketball team did not get on the front page that day. Their score was there; but their article was in the back of the paper. You are on the front page!"

Then I found out that – though I had been miles away and could not comfort my wife – over 140 people had been there at the hospital with her. There were Christian doctors who explained things to her and helped her. They were with my son and my wife all the way. They got Matt admitted to Riley Hospital.

There were Christian doctors from Indianapolis University coming to see Matt, Christian doctors from Riley, and Christian nurses. Everybody was concerned about him. Do you see what I see? I am just so glad I am a part of the family of God. The head anesthesiologist told me, "When your son gets operated on, I have signed up. I am going to be in there with him." He is a Christian. A Christian lady who works in the recovery room said, "I will work late the night your son is operated on because I want to be in there with him."

During the operation, just about everyone in the operating room was Christian. Do you see what I see? God is at work answering all those prayers. This is the Body of Christ. I did not put any signs on the door saying, "No white Christians allowed." I was just glad to be part of the family. God was doing a mighty work.

The Reconciliation Event

I see Satan seeking to divide the family. Sharon and I took turns as we stayed with Matt 24 hours a day. From the hospital, I started doing email updates to send out over the Internet to keep some con-cerned, praying people informed. People began to pray all across America, all across the world. I still get emails from all over the world!

One night when I was with Matt, he awakened me with a request, "Can you pray for me?"

"What do you want me to pray for?" I asked.

"I am scared," he responded. "I have been having this dream about white people calling black people the n-word, and fighting going on, and wanting to kill myself."

I said, "Son, that is nothing but the devil. You are the reconciliation event in Indianapolis right now. Black people, white people, yellow people, even Brad Schaaf was here today telling me in sign language that the deaf churches are praying for you."

Shine, Saints, Shine! The Shining Light of Family Love

God is working among His people. Our personal deacon took over everything. He said, "We want to help you with anything we can. We have people lined up at our church. Anything you need – just say it, and you've got it."

The outpouring was overwhelming. Kimber Kauffman, my pastor (who happens to be white), had to make a statement to the church, "Please stop bringing food to the Wares. They cannot eat all that food. Bring it to the church. We'll freeze it, and they can get it when they want. However, we will need a freezer. Will somebody donate one?" Before the day was over, three freezers had been offered. I asked them not to collect *that* much food.

I found that God is capable of doing a supernatural work. I had returned home concerned about money and all the rest. But God was working beyond my ability to ask or think. I learned that Heritage Christian School, where my son was a student, Baptist Bible College, where I am the president, and College Park Baptist Church, where I am a member and an elder, had been discussing a Matt Ware Trust Fund. They asked me what I thought about it. I told them, "I do not even understand it; but just do not do anything that would impinge upon my ministry." They put a CPA on the planning team. They put a lawyer and business people on it. They met, and they set it up.

People asked me, "What do you need?"

I told them, "I do not know." I told my wife, "This thing is so big. I cannot even figure it out; we will just live one day at a time."

A brother called me to let me know, "Brother Ware, if you need any money, we have $20,000 in the trust fund."

I said, "That is amazing!"

The reporter who ran the first article in the *Star* wrote another article that hit front page again! A thought occurs to me that I did not even think about at the time. The Lord had brought us another miracle: That day there were two black men on the front page of the *Indianapolis Star*, and they had not robbed or raped anybody. Do you see what I see?

The trust fund treasurer called to update me again, "Money is coming into the fund. It is up to about $44,000. Do you want me to post this on the church web site?"

I said, "Sure, go right ahead."

My pastor made another appeal, "Now listen, folks. We have got to do something for the Ware family." So, once a year in December, we usually take up an offering — not just an offering — ALL monies that come in, tithes, offering, EVERYTHING that comes in we give away to ministry. This past year, we gave $70,000 on that Sunday. Pastor said, "This year, April 19 is Matt Ware Day. ALL monies that come in here will go to the Matt Ware Trust Fund."

I told my wife, "Man, I do not know what these people are doing, but they will probably get $40,000 to $50,000. If you fantasize, they may get about $70,000." The day came, and they took the money up that night. Matt went to the first service. Some of the money came from nonmembers, but it came through our church. It came in, and I was not even there. I had to leave to speak at another service, come back, pick Matt up, and take him back to the hospital.

Somebody said, "God blessed this wonderful service."

I said, "Praise God."

They asked, "Do you know the total of the offering?"

I said, "No, I do not."

They said, "It was $165,000!"

Do you see what I see? God began to deal with me, "Listen, you were on that plane talking about working two or three jobs. I have your back covered, Buddy."

I see heaven's host intrigued by the spread of faith. Do you see what I see? I asked my son, "Matt, what does it feel like to be a heavenly celebrity? With so many people praying for you around the world, the angels are probably asking God, 'Who is this Matt Ware kid? They are praying for him all over the place.' Now I want you to understand. That is miraculous."

I thought about it and thought, "What would I have to do get the whole world praying for my family?" I could not figure it out. However, I think God was saying something to me. As I told Matt, "I would much rather serve God out of my strength, but sometimes God puts us in a weak position that He may demonstrate His power."

Moreover, the witness of this is going out all over. I walked in the bank to make a deposit. The teller looked up and said, "That's Matt Ware's dad – he's the kid everybody is talking about, right? He is the one who got injured. He goes to Heritage Christian School."

I walked into the post office; and a lady said, "Hey, yeah, I have been praying for your son."

I told Matt, "If this thing keeps up, boy, you are going to have to pay me for being your agent." It is miraculous. It is something that God is just blowing my mind with. I can go on and on; but all I am trying to say is this: I do believe in the people of God in a moment of crisis. When we have sown seeds, tried to love, and tried to hold onto our integrity, they will come through for us.

Eternal Values – What Really Matters

When Matt got hurt, I began to ask, "How do I really want to spend my life anyway?" A lot of things did not matter any more. A lot of things we used to fuss and fight about, I could care less about. I raised the question to myself, "Do you even want to be involved in that kind of stuff anymore? You have higher priorities. You have things to think about. You have places to go and things to do. Your traveling schedule is going to be cut down. You have a son to take care of. Are those things REALLY important?"

Then God helped me. He said, *Just think about what has happened.*

Some people hit me with that, too. They said; "You have been sowing seeds. You have been preaching to blacks. You have been preaching to whites. You have been reaching out to the deaf."

I was beginning to think sometimes, "God, does it really mean anything? I am preaching here. I am preaching there. Is it really accomplishing anything?"

I believe God is using this illustration to say, "Son, you have been sowing seeds, and now it is harvest time. You have been made weak that I can give you a glimpse of my power."

I see the people of God coming around one family, reconciled. That has been deeply encouraging. I meditated before God and came to this conclusion: As long as an opportunity is Biblical — as long as it is right — I am going to take this little light of mine, and I am going to let it shine until Jesus comes. I am going to let it shine among white believers, among black believers, among yellow believers, and among red believers. I am going to do my best to let this little light shine all over the place until Jesus comes.

Do you see what I see? I am humbled at this time. It does not matter what anybody says because I have higher things on my mind now. I am not concerned about whether you sway, whether you say amen, or whether you clap. I do not care if you sit there quietly in the pew. I do not care! What I care about are people who know Jesus — people who know the lordship of Christ — people who can get a hold of Christ — people who can be a part of the family of God and help us go forth for the glory of God. I just say shine, Saints, shine. Let this world see our good works. I see the empty hands of faith receiving the power of God through the family.

After I had been in that hospital Thursday through Sunday, on Monday morning I got a call from the public relations people at Riley Hospital. They said, "The media has been calling all weekend about your son. We have kept them away. It is your decision. If you want to talk to the media, let us know. If you do not, we will tell them there is no comment. They cannot come into this hospital without proper authorization."

I said to the lady, "If they want to talk about the accident and what happened, I have nothing more to say. But if they want to talk about the faith of our family and the faith of the Christian community, we are ready to talk." I want to tell you, every article that they have presented has been an article of faith. Every editorial they have done has been one of faith. This little light of mine, I am going to let it shine. I do not mind telling you that white people prayed for me. Black people prayed for me. Yellow prayed for me. Deaf people prayed for me. Poor people prayed for me. Rich people prayed for me. God's people prayed for me! Shine, saints, shine.

I thank the Father that Jesus is the Light of the world that lights all of us. I trust that every one of you has been lit by the regenerative work of Jesus Christ. I trust that we are allowing the light to shine, that others are seeing the light, and that because of it, they are singing the praises, not of men, but of God, our Father. We praise God; we thank Him that we are part of the family of God. In addition, we say to all of our brothers and sisters, "Welcome to the family. May God be glorified."

2 – Lights in a Dark World

A. Charles Ware[□]

I recommend that all Christians read *Our Racist Legacy*[1], written by Ivan A. Beals, a white Christian. *Our Racist Legacy* views the struggle from a historical perspective. Beals does a good job of documenting one of the things blacks need to understand in the discussion of slavery, discrimination, and Jim Crowism. He brings out the fact that – while so many whites were on the wrong side of the issue – there were many who were on the right side as well. We have to give the Quakers and others their due for their stand against slavery. We have to give recognition to those churches which split over the slave issue before the Civil War. We have to give those white people their place who went in and taught blacks when it was against the law. There were those who got involved in the Underground Railroad, who helped bring blacks to freedom. We have to give them their place because truth must be honored.

[□] Dr. A. Charles Ware is president of Baptist Bible College of Indianapolis. The founder of the Voice of Biblical Reconciliation, he is a tireless advocate for multiracial ministry.

[1] Ivan A. Beals. (1997). *Our racist legacy: Will the church resolve the conflict?* Notre Dame, Indiana: Cross Cultural Publications.

White Light in a Dark World

Our Racist Legacy is so powerful because Beals goes back to the records of the major denominational meetings and gives you what they said in their minutes – some bad, but some good. He quotes from the sermons of the preachers of the era – some bad, some good. We need to understand our history correctly because – as I said in my book, *Prejudice and the People of God* – what I am concerned about ultimately is truth. My concern is for what is Biblical and what is right. Christians should be committed to racial reconciliation rooted in redemption.

This chapter is not written to the world. It is written to people who have been regenerated, who have been born again, who are part of the Family of God. Even though I am talking to Bible-believing people now, I feel led to emphasize again for the record that reconciliation must be rooted in redemption and guided by revelation – that is, by the Word of God. This chapter is a continuation of my first chapter in this book because I do not think that all Christians see the same things.

The True Source of Light Is the Bible

I am passionate about the racial reconciliation issue because I believe it to be Biblical. That is why I am committed to it. It is almost incomprehensible that there are people who say there is no problem. I want to ask them, "Do you see what I see?" Christians have promoted segregation on the basis that it was the will of God as revealed in the Word of God. In my book, I go over some of the Scriptures that people have interpreted incorrectly. First, there are passages which some claim teach against interracial marriage:

Genesis 11, the Tower of Babel.

Genesis 9 and 10, the so-called Hamitic curse, the curse that was really on Canaan.

All the Scriptures to Israel about not intermarrying with strange women.

Scriptures in Proverbs about strange women.

I go over those Scriptures and teach people what those passages say in their context because what I see is a racist history, especially among fundamental, evangelical Bible believers. Some who have not given thought to the topic may be surprised to learn that in the name of God, we separated, creating unholy schisms in the Body of Christ. In addition, there are many fundamental, evangelical believers who would say,

I do not see anything wrong with black people; they need to get saved just like anybody else. They should have a right to get a job just like anybody else. But when it comes to living in my community, that would be going a little far. God said He wanted the races separated. Therefore, we need a black school and a white school. We need a black church and a white church. We need a black college and a white college.

It was all based upon *misinterpretation* that led to *misapplication* that led to *misdirection*. In case you do not know it, we have many people in our churches who still believe that way.

A Contemporary Topic – Darkness Persists to This Hour. When I went through these same Scriptures in a recent class at Baptist Bible College, a student in the back of the room raised his hand and said,

> I just want to say that everything the president has said is true. Before I came to Baptist Bible College, I was a member of a church right here in Indiana that taught me every one of those Scriptures. They told me the black man has a smaller brain, that the black man is inferior, and that interracial marriage is wrong.

This demonstrates just how contemporary the topic is. As I preach in churches, I sometimes ask myself, "Why am I still talking about this stuff? It's past; it's gone." It requires a constant effort to resist being lulled into the prevailing sense of complacency which rules so much of Christendom.

Too often Christians teach erroneous doctrine without critical evaluation of the presuppositions which have been pounded into them over decades by equally unthinking leaders. For example, I preached on the Hamitic curse at a church once, and the pastor's wife came up to me afterward. What she said to me caused me to feel embarrassment for the pastor because he is a good man of the Word. The pastor's wife said, "I am glad you clarified the matter about the Hamitic curse. One of the Sunday school teachers taught our kids the erroneous teaching just two weeks ago." Do you see what I see? The church is rampant with error. It is sometimes surprising where the error rears its ugly head. That's why we must be vigilant.

Both Blacks and Whites Need Some Light

We must always pray and not faint. I encounter black people who say, "We are giving up, the white people will not come to the table. We cannot relate to one another."

I encounter white people who say essentially the same thing, "Brother Ware, we tried reconciliation, and blacks will not come to the meetings."

I ask both groups if they want to be models to the world. Do we want them to know that Jesus Christ is the Son of God? Do we want them to know that we are the people of God?

Bright Lights in a Troubled World. There are Christians who cannot sit down and have a civilized discussion about the race issue. They get just as mad at each other as worldly people. I do not doubt that they probably would curse just like the world. I am seeing trouble. People tell me, "No, no, no! There is no trouble; that's all settled."

However, I see new trouble everyday; and I continue to say, "Whoa, wait a minute. There is plenty trouble right here in the Christian family."

We still have to deal with the text in Matthew 5, the Sermon on the Mount, where we are commanded to let our light shine. It is not a suggestion. In Matthew 5:13, the Bible says,

> You are the salt of the earth, but if the salt has lost its savor, wherewith shall it be salted. It is thenceforth good for nothing but to be cast out and to be trodden under foot of men.

Jesus uses two metaphors to make His point. In the first instance, He says we are salt. There are many interpretations about what salt represents. The best is that salt is a preservative. Salt stops decay.

Some may not realize it, but we are living in a decaying society. In this society, I am seeing morals go out the window. Violence is on the increase. I am seeing polarization and hatred. I am seeing people who do not know right from wrong. They do wrong and think they are doing right.

According to Romans 1, mankind is not evolving – we are devolving. We are going DOWN-hill, not UP the hill. In discussions of race relations in this new millennium, the 1990s will be considered the generation of separation. Nonetheless, in the midst of this decaying society, the Church is supposed to be a preservative. We are supposed to be salt.

Pass the Salt, Please – Calling on God to Stop the Decay

When God was going to destroy Sodom and Gomorrah, Abraham was there pleading with Him. Abraham did not pray, "But God, if we could just get one Christian into the White House, would you spare Sodom and Gomorrah?" No! He did not negotiate, "God, if we could just put more money into public education, would you spare the cities?" That wasn't the argument. That is not salt. The salt is in the Church. Instead, Abraham asked, "God, if there are fifty *righteous* people, would you spare Sodom and Gomorrah?"

God replied, "For fifty 'salt-shakers,' I'll spare the cities."

Wanting to improve his odds, Abraham continued, "God, okay, if we do not have fifty, suppose there are forty, just forty 'salts,' would you preserve that land?"

Again, God was willing to extend mercy to two entire cities on the basis of one saint's petition and the existence of a small body of believers.

Emboldened by God's willingness to enter into serious dialogue with His servant, Abraham kept reducing the number of righteous persons until he finally asked, "Hmm, oh God, please don't be angry with me; but what about ten?"

God graciously conceded, "For ten, I'll spare the cities." I can't fault Abraham for thinking that perhaps he had struck a bargain with God that would save a lot of people from suffering. What Abraham failed to reckon with, however, is that there were not ten righteous people to be found in all the twin cities.

This is a parable for our times. The world is decaying. They do not have the answer. Why are we running to them? Why are we listening to them? The Church tries to mimic the world too much, and we get the same results the world gets. (One definition of insanity is doing the same thing over and over and expecting different results.) It is about time to get back to the Book. Do you see what I see? You can't show me in the Book where our culture is greater than our Christ. People talk about Afrocentrism; I talk about Christocentrism. People talk about returning to their roots, but they will not dig deeply enough. If they keep digging, they are going to find Adam. That is where their roots are. That is where my roots are.

The Church has been invaded by the world. We are no longer salt. We are no longer capable of preserving anything. In fact, sometimes the world looks at us and gives us the ultimate condemnation, "Who are you to criticize us? You are worse off than we are." To make matters worse, we try to excuse our behavior with the Word of God.

We are supposed to be not only salt, but also light. Verse 14 makes a simple but profound declaration of fact, "You are the light of the world." The Church cannot expect the world to guide us. We must look to the Word to guide us.

Do You Have a Light? Are You Reflecting the True Light? Jesus drives home His point by adding, "A city that is set on a hill cannot be hid. Neither do men light a candle and put it under a bushel, but under a candlestick, and it gives light to all who are in the house." What type of light are we giving in the area of racial relations?

In verse 15 he adds, "Let your light so shine before men that they may see your good works and glorify your Father which is in heaven." I do not talk about racial reconciliation just because it is a good work. Again, as I attempted to say in *Prejudice and the People of God,* racial reconciliation is important Biblically because of the redemption of Christ and because of related teachings in the Bible. We are told in Ephesians 4:3 "Endeavor to keep the unity of the Spirit in the bond of peace." Unity is a good work. Paul says in 2 Corinthians 5 that you and I have been given the ministry of reconciliation. I am trying to lead all mankind to see what is the unity and the wisdom that God created when He bought the Jew and the Gentile and made them one. This is a good work.

In other words, we have to let our light shine in such a way that people can see it. They do not see your good attitude; they see your good works. They do not see your good doctrine. They see the demonstration of that doctrine in your life. Let them see your good works, and the result will be that they are going to praise our Father. We want the world to sing the praises of our God, do we not? Do you see what I see? I do not see a world that is singing the praises of our Father. I see a world that is cursing our Father, in part, because they see injustice perpetrated by those who claim to be His children. The remedy is simple. We have to let our little light shine.

Sparks in the Night: The Saints Are Beginning to Shine

There are four applications I would like to make about letting our lights shine. First, we need some sparks in the night. When you shoot up a little spark in pitch-black darkness, you can see it clearly – like a lightning bug. As people look out into the night, without any warning they can see one here and one there. Instead of sparks in the night, however, what we see is discouraging. We do not see many churches dealing with this issue; so many of the rest of us get discouraged. We think nothing is going on. However, I want to tell you that every once in a while I see a spark in the night.

I thank God that when I look at Armitage Baptist Church and Pastor Charles Lyons of Chicago, I can say, "There is a spark in the night."

For another example, Dr. Paul Dixon has said that he grew up in the South. So did I. Dr. Dixon said to our conference attendees, "When the civil rights struggle was going on, I was on the other side. I passed by. I was on the wrong side." That is a spark in the night.

Some of us got upset – in fact, I got upset, too – when I read an article that people thought to be newsworthy. It seems that a black person died in a small southern town in 1997. His church did not have enough room to hold all the people who wanted to honor his memory. Because they were bigger, a white church opened their doors to allow black people to come to the funeral of the black man. The article said that what made this deed so strange was that this was the first time blacks were ever allowed in that sanctuary. Now, on the one hand, I got mad and said, *this is 1997. What do you mean? And you claim to be Christians?* However, I also looked at that act and saw it as a spark in the night.

When I was in Mississippi in January 1998, some people told me about local churches that still have in their constitution that a black man cannot come into their sanctuary. Are these attitudes still extant in 1998? For sure! Somebody is talking to these churches now. Mission Mississippi is a statewide ministry addressing racial reconciliation. That is a spark in the night.

Some may object, "But I do not want a spark." Based on my experience, I have learned that you have to start somewhere. The Mississippi dialogues represent a spark in the night. Jesus is working. Churches are beginning to deal with the past and confess they were Biblically wrong back then. They want to change now, open up, and invite people in. In the face of all this, some of us get mad and say, "I do not want to come. You waited this long? Forget it." Some of us need to understand that we weren't even born when those churches were closed. Therefore, we could not have gone to them anyway. Accept these sparks in the night. They have to change somewhere, somehow. We have to let that light shine.

Jesus lit that spark. Consider the history of some of these individuals who are making these changes. They never would have changed unless they were born again, unless somebody confronted them with the Word of God, and unless somebody confronted them with their past history. They are sparks in the night. Jesus is at work in their good works. I agree, the scenario is dismal in places, but there are sparks in the night.

While we must accept the sparks in the night, we nevertheless need to let our own light shine so that it can be seen and cause people to praise our Father.

Torches in the Night: The Saints Are Getting Hot. Not only do we need sparks, we also need some flames in the night. One of those flames is Brother Charles Lyons. Lyons is a white man in the inner city of Chicago doing a work with people from some 37 nations. He is a white man living in a community where there is gang warfare going on. As the gangs were shooting it out on one occasion, one of the bullets strayed and killed a three-year-old who was riding a tricycle in the vicinity. When the funeral was held for the three-year-old, members from both gangs were in attendance.

Brother Charles Lyons stood up in his pulpit at that funeral, and he told both gangs, "There is no need for you to blame the other gang; you are both wrong! Your lifestyle of violence is leading to innocent people dying. You need to repent of your sin and come to Jesus."

Brother Lyons let his light shine so that men might see his good works and glorify his Father in heaven. He preached a powerful sermon that day. The Holy Spirit moved mightily. The Chicago Tribune put the sermon on the front page. The reporter observed, "This is Charles Lyons' turf. He lives here. He jogs here. He preaches here. This is his congregation."

There are some flames out there. Flames in the night. While I see people struggling against God, I also see God doing something in the hearts of His people.

People quite often ask me,

Are you encouraged or discouraged? Where do you think reconciliation is going? We have had Promise Keepers. We have had this. We have had other pro-grams. Do you think it is going forward or do you think it is going backward?

One thing that I see is that God is touching the hearts of His people. There are people who at least want to talk about racial reconciliation. When I was in school, you could not even talk about it. If you raised the race issue, they called you a communist, a rebel, or worse. But they would not discuss the issue. Back then, people suffered injustices; they were humiliated. I spoke with an individual who had had his leg amputated early in life. He has gone through most of

his life as a handicapped individual. He told me
recently,

> I have attended school with my handicap. I have
> played ball as a handicapper. But I have never been
> made to feel so little – I have never been humiliated so
> much – as when I spent a semester in a fundamental,
> Bible-believing, Christian college. All because I am black.

In spite of all that, God is still raising up some
flames. There are people who are burning with
passion – black people, white people, brown people,
and yellow people who are beginning to be ignited by
the Word of God. Christ has my life. I am no longer
submitted to our traditions or our heritage. I am now
submitted to our Lord who told us, "By this shall all
men know that you are my disciples, in that you have
love one for another."

There are organizations, Christian colleges, and
denominations that are beginning to talk about
diversity and to have diversity study groups and
diversity meetings. Ken Hutcherson serves as senior
pastor of Antioch Bible Church, a multiracial congregation, located outside of Seattle, with over 3000 in
attendance. Antioch plans to start 15 other multiracial
churches. Flames are beginning to burn because
some people are simply saying that racial reconciliation is the Biblical thing to do. We cannot deny it. We
have to do something about it. I praise God for that.

Some black folk resent the notion of total
integration. Their feeling is that anytime you integrate,
the white folk take over. My question is, *Are we that
insecure?* What God has for me, no one can take. I

do not care if they are white, black, or polka dot. I happen to believe in the sovereignty of God.

People ask, "Are you a black leader?" No, I am a Christian leader. I am going to lead people who are Christian who want to follow the Book.

There are flames in the night. There was a time in the early days of America when a black person could pastor a white church, and that was all right. Then we got emancipated and everybody got segregated. For quite a while after that, white people would not consider having a black pastor for anything.

I have pastored a predominantly white church and I have pastored a predominantly black church. I speak in some white churches where they do not have pastors, and they want to know if I want to put my name in as a candidate. Some people say that can not be done. I beg to differ. There are some flames in the night.

In fact, I remember a church where I preached on three occasions. After the first sermon, as people were shaking my hand, I was touched when a little white boy of about 12 years of age asked, "Can I ask you one question?"

I said, "Sure, young man. What would you like to know?"

"Can you be our next pastor?" he asked.

I chuckled and said, "No, man. That is all right."

When I came back to preach on a subsequent occasion, the same little fellow asked me again, "Will you consider being our pastor now?"

Pleased with his continued high esteem of my preaching gifts, I nonetheless had to decline. I chuckled again and said, "No, man. I have things to do and places to go."

The third time I went to that church, the little fellow came up to me again. That time he said, "I have only got one thing to say."

"What's that?" I asked.

He responded, "If you cannot be our pastor, I am sure praying that God will send us somebody just like you."

The Saints Are Getting Brighter. Happily, some things are changing. In fact, black people are getting to be a commodity. I hear white folk all over complaining, "We cannot get black professors. We cannot get black teachers. We cannot get black members."

Black is gold for some white people right now. When they come around my college, I tell them, "I am not giving you any of my black teachers. I need my own teachers." Things are changing now.

Not only are black preachers and teachers in demand, so are white leaders who understand what the Word says about loving one another. A black pastor called me and asked,

> Brother Ware, who have you got coming out of BBCI? I mean, who have you got white coming out of BBCI? I am a black pastor, and I want a white associate. Do you have anybody coming out of there that understands racial reconciliation who can partner with me in leadership?

I never used to get that kind of call.

Some Questions Remain. Some of my brothers criticize me for asking some hard questions. I don't care. When people ask me to come to our college to tell our students about their mission program, I ask them,

> Are there any fields black people cannot go to? Tell me now, so I can tell my students before you get there so you do not have to stand there and lie when you say, "There's a BIG world out there, and God needs missionaries. Come join our team." The black students may come forth. For too many years, they have heard mission executives respond, "Why, yes. You would work real well in the inner cities of America."

When they have said, "No, no, no, we want to go to Africa, Asia, Europe," or some other fertile mission field, the recruiters have seemed incredulous, "You want to go to where? You cannot do anything in Africa. You look too much like the Africans."

I ask them how they know that similar physical characteristics will not help. That's why I want to know what restrictions exist before they even come to BBCI. A lot of this hemming and hawing just serves to perpetuate a color-coded segregation. Thank God, however, flames are beginning to burn.

I run into so many blacks who have been the first black in their organizations. They often leave with bitter feelings. Many develop the feeling that the white people they worked with are too insensitive. I have heard comments like, "You will not believe their rules and policies. You will not believe how ignorant they are." But I thank God. They are flames in the night.

Part of the training of some of the individuals in our institutions, black and white, involves racial *sensitivity* or *awareness*. Ken Davis teaches a course called Race, Culture, and the Church. Every student who goes through our college has to take it because we want them to go out and be flames in the night. We want to develop people who are going to stand square and ask one question, "What does the Bible say?" We'll take our stand on the Book.

Celebration. What I am praying for is a display like Fourth of July fireworks. I want to hear a spectacular BOOM! I want to get to the place where we are letting our light so shine that it is being seen by men so that they begin praising our Father all across America. I want to see it in small country towns, in the depths of the inner city, and out in the suburbs. I want to see it where God's people are loving God's people. Then all across this nation people will begin saying,

> These people are free indeed. They have been delivered from their sin. They can talk to one another. They can love one another, worship with one another, and learn from one another. What is it about this thing called the Church?

That is real independence, when God sets you free from your selfishness, bigotry, and sin – when God sets you free from your desire to be comfortable and conform everybody to your image. Freedom comes when God teaches you to consider others better than yourself – when God teaches you that you are not here to be served, but to serve. I tell our students, "I want you to be multicultural. I want you to be able to function in any situation for the glory of God."

Christ Over Culture

It is somewhat perplexing how people allow racism and culture to crowd Christ from His place of preeminence. Some refuse to go to churches where they will not be in the majority. They let culture dictate their spirituality. On the one hand, some white people tell me, "You preach too loudly." On the other hand, some black folks say, "You are not loud enough. Why don't you get loose?"

I tell both groups, "What you see is what you get." The bottom line is, "We should want the Word." As old Preacher Brown used to tell his congregation, "I do not care how high you jump. What I am concerned about is how straight you walk when you come down."

The issue is holiness. You may say, "Amen" to punctuate each of the preacher's phrases; or you may be as quiet as a peep. In the final analysis, the real issue is, does the Word light your soul and bring forth good works to be seen of men that they may glorify your Father? Anything that does not produce good works is not worth its salt.

Your light can shine in unexpected ways. I am praying to God about my son Matt's spinal injury and about his light. I thank God how his accident is being used to glorify God. A lot of Matt's brightness is a result of effort by Christians on the inside of various organizations. Matt received a jersey from the Indianapolis Pacers. It is the real McCoy! It has his name on the back, along with his number 12. I told him, "Man, they have you on the team. Go in there and get a paycheck this season."

Matt went to a Pacers game. Someone arranged for all the Pacers to autograph a basketball and a cap for Matt. He also received a Pacer warm-up uniform. He got a card from the Philadelphia 76ers autographed by all the players. Matt has received cards from nursery schools, third grades, high schools, colleges, and churches. He has received email from all over. Even brother Rob Elkington said, "Matt's injury has affected my church. We have been changed in South Africa because of your son." Yes, I am looking for a Fourth-of-July-like celebration. Rob Elkington also mentioned to me that,

> The Church in post-apartheid South Africa wants to be lit by Jesus. We want to let our light shine so that other South Africans can see our good works and praise our Father in heaven; and we want to make a network with the Church in America.

Sadly, I had to reply, "Rob, I apologize. But I really do not feel we have much to say. Our light is not shining too well." What are we going to tell the South Africans? I really do not know. I would like to see that Fourth of July stuff spread wherever God's people can be found.

Finally, I am looking for that bright sunshiny day – no, that bright S-O-N-shiny day. I am looking for the day when I'll be caught up to meet the Lord in the air, when I'll be ushered into the presence of the Lord in heaven. I am looking for that day when our heritage will not matter, when our color will not matter, when our class will not matter. What will matter is that we are in the presence of the Son of God. All prejudice will be removed. We'll be humble as we ought to be, and He'll be the center of our attention. In heaven, every tongue shall confess, and every knee shall bow. We will call him Lord of Lords and King of Kings. We are his children. We are family. I am looking for that bright Son-shiny day.

I know where I am going. I am just trying to prepare. When some Christians get to heaven, they are going to be shocked, saying, "I didn't know you people would be up here. I thought for sure there would be a west side and an east side of heaven."

My Dream

They might as well get ready now. Somebody asked me once, "Brother Ware, what are you trying to accomplish through this reconciliation stuff anyway? I mean, what is it you really want?"

I said, "If I broke it down to one thing, it would be simply this: for my life and for the saints, I would merely want us to look at one another through the eyes of Jesus Christ. If He is the light that lights the world – if by regeneration He has lit you – then you should allow Him to shine through. When they can see more of Jesus and less of us, that is when they will see our good works and glorify our Father who is in heaven. Do you see what I see? I see a world that is crumbling.

As I wrote in *Prejudice and the People of God*, truth DOES matter. I am hearing some Christians say, "Truth doesn't matter. We just need to reconcile." Truth DOES matter! What I say and do, I am saying and doing because it is the truth. When Christians are wishy-washy, they get scared to read their Bible because they are afraid they might disagree with another Christian. When you stand before God, He is not going to ask you what other Christians believed. He is going to ask you what you did in response to His Word. So, we had better study to show ourselves workmen approved unto God who need not be ashamed, rightly dividing the Word of Truth. Let your light so shine before men that they may see your good works and glorify your Father in heaven.

Are you a spark? Are you a flame? Are you one of those individuals trying to give us that Fourth of July extravaganza? I want a beautiful plethora of colors and cultures at Baptist Bible College of Indianapolis so that when people come, they may say that this is the way heaven looks. That is where we are going – looking for that bright Son-shiny day. Pray with me that God will empower us to let our lights shine on this earth:

Father, we thank you for your love. Thank you for the Word of God. Thank you for the people of God. We pray that you might work in our lives in such a way that we might be models. In some places the spark is just beginning. In some places, flames have been established. Our desire is that we might be a part of a great racial reconciliation Fourth of July celebration. And God, our hearts long for and we look for that blessed hope when we will be caught up with Jesus and made like Him. In His name, we pray. Amen.

3 – Racial Reconciliation in Genesis

Ken Ham[⊞]

What does Genesis have to do with racial reconciliation? We will address that question in this chapter. Our organization, *Answers in Genesis*, is committed to defending the authority of Genesis, the first book in the Bible.

Marrying Your Relative

Here is a test question for you.

1. Can you marry your relative?

   ❑ Yes?

   ❑ No?

   ❑ Probably?

   ❑ Only after counseling?

[⊞] Australian-born Ken Ham is founder and executive director of the Bible-defending ministry of Answers in Genesis-USA, located near Cincinnati. He is a frequent conference speaker, prolific author, and host of a daily radio program "Answers ... with Ken Ham."

Actually, let me put it this way: If you are married, take a look at your wife (or husband). If she were not related to you before you married her, then you did not marry a human! When you get married, you have to marry a relative. The Bible teaches that all human beings go back to one man and one woman – Adam and Eve. Therefore, we are *all* related.

In Romans 5:12, Paul tells us, "Wherefore as by one man (the first man, Adam), sin entered the world and death by sin, and so death passed upon all men, for all have sinned." Since we are all descendants of Adam, we are all sinners; and we are all under the judgment of death. When you think about it, that puts all of us on an even keel, does it not?

Lost Worlds. Let me ask another question as we jump from Adam to dinosaurs. There is a connection between dinosaurs and racial reconciliation. Are you familiar with those movies, *Jurassic Park* or *Lost World* – you know, those evolutionary, New Age, humanistic, atheistic, anti-God movies? Well, I saw them, too, but for research purposes only, of course.

Tyrannosaurus Rex is that great big dinosaur with teeth up to six inches long. Another question:

2. How would Tyrannosaurus Rex originally have been described?

    ❑ Plant-eater?

    ❑ Meat-eater?

    ❑ Scavenger?

    ❑ Plant- and meat-eater?

I want to start with the Bible, God's Word; and I want to build our thinking on the Bible. I want to take God's Word the way that Jesus Christ, who is the living Word, did. In fact, how did Jesus Christ take the book of Genesis? In Matthew 19:4-6, when asked about divorce, Jesus said,

> Have you not read, He which made them in the beginning made them male and female and said "for this cause shall a man leave his father and mother and cleave unto his wife and the twain will be one flesh"?

From where did Jesus quote? Genesis. In fact, He quoted from Genesis 1 and Genesis 2. What He was saying was, if we want to understand marriage, we have to understand Genesis because marriage is founded in Genesis. Jesus believed Genesis as literal history. In fact, a married couple becomes one because they are one flesh. Eve was taken out of Adam. The reason it is one man for one woman for life is because God made a man and a woman. He did not make a man and a man, or a woman and a woman. He made a man and a woman – a literal man and woman in history.

Churches that condone homosexual behavior or ordaining homosexual pastors, I guarantee, do not believe in a literal Genesis. As soon as you believe in a literal Genesis, it is one man for one woman for life.

Not only that, there are many Christians who ask, "Why can't you believe in evolution? Why can't Christians believe that man evolved over millions of years?"

There are many Christians who try to "add" God to evolution. They have man coming from an ape-man, and woman coming from an ape-woman. If man and woman have separate ancestries like that, you destroy the whole basis of oneness because they would not be of one blood. You destroy the family. What Jesus is teaching here is that the literal history of Genesis is foundational to marriage and an understanding of the meaning of marriage.

But not just marriage. Ultimately every single Biblical doctrine of theology, either directly or indirectly, is founded in the book of Genesis? For example, in Genesis 1-11, we find the following:

- ❑ Sin
- ❑ Death
- ❑ Why Jesus died on a cross
- ❑ Dominion
- ❑ Work
- ❑ Why we have a seven-day week
- ❑ Why Jesus is called the last Adam
- ❑ Clothing
- ❑ And more

Ultimately, every single Biblical doctrine of theology is found in the book of Genesis, either directly or indirectly, especially in the first eleven chapters. It blows my mind to think that so many Christians say Genesis does not matter, when in fact Genesis 1-11 is foundational to the rest of the Bible. Unless we believe and understand Genesis 1-11 and defend it aggressively, we have no foundation for the rest of the Bible. Furthermore, we will have no foundation for a Christian worldview.

If you take Genesis in the same straightforward way that Jesus took Genesis, without any outside influences whatsoever, Genesis 1:29-30 teaches that originally Adam and Eve were vegetarians, and the animals were vegetarians. This is substantiated by Genesis 9:3, where God said to Noah after the flood, "Now, I give you the animals to eat, just as I gave you the plants."

Therefore, if you devoured a turkey for supper, that is okay. It would not have been okay before sin, however. Before sin, there was no death (of animals or man) in the world. In fact, if you take Genesis to Revelation consistently, interpreting Scripture with Scripture, and not taking any outside ideas from the world to the Bible, but studying solely from the Bible, the Bible teaches adamantly that there was a perfect world. When Adam rebelled, sin came into the world; and that changed everything. As a result, death, bloodshed, disease, thorns, and suffering entered the universe.

Some individuals still have a problem here. There are many Christians who believe in an Earth that is millions of years old because the fossil record is said to be millions of years old. Note that the fossil record is full of dead bones. If you believe that dinosaurs died out millions of years ago, you would have death, disease (because there *is* disease in those bones), suffering, and bloodshed before Adam sinned. If the Bible says Adam's sin brought death, disease, bloodshed, and suffering, could there have been disease (like cancer) in the world before sin?

Sin and Racial Reconciliation

An understanding of the origin of sin – what sin really is, and sin's consequences – is prerequisite to resolving anything to do with racial reconciliation. We have to understand our very nature and what has happened in this universe.

By the way, some people say, "Wait a minute, didn't plants die before Adam sinned?" Yes, of course. Actually, plants were given for food, but plants do not have that *nephesh*. In Genesis 1, the Hebrew word that applies to man and animals is *nephesh*, a life spirit that animals and men have that plants do not have. Plants are not "living" in the same sense that animals are.

All of us, unfortunately, have been "evolutionized," to coin a word. That is one of the reasons we have so many problems trying to sort out the difficulties we encounter in understanding Genesis. By "evolution-ized," I mean that our schools assume that evolution is true as a point of departure for so much of the education we receive. The media assumes the truth of evolution in its reporting of scientific phenomena. Our language of ordinary discourse incorporates the evolutionary worldview subconsciously.

Many will object, "But I don't believe in evolution I do not believe that molecules turned into people over millions of years." However, that is *not* what evolution is all about. There is a popular idea that molecules turned into some sort of living system millions of years ago. Then one kind of animal evolved into another, then into yet another. Later on, ape-like creatures turned into an early pre-man. Finally, you got your average garden-variety human.

I hate to shock you; but that is not evolution, per sé. That is really the *mechanism* that Darwin popularized to try to defend the idea that life arose without God. Evolution is much, much more than this. Evolution is a whole philosophy of life that teaches that man determines truth by himself, independent of God.

Again, one of the problems is that we have been immersed in an education system and saturated by a media which leads us to assume a starting point outside the Bible. Unconsciously, many of us regard the Bible as an interesting book of stories, if you will. It is a book about salvation and religion. However, we have a number of other ideas that we learned in biology and geology. We try to add those ideas to the Bible. That is one of the reasons why many people do not approach the problems in our culture in the right way. Instead of starting with the Bible as foundational to our thinking, we start outside the Bible, take those ideas to the Bible, and wonder why we cannot solve the problems.

Many people might say, "Now wait a minute. You are saying there was no death before sin? What about animals such as that South American monkey, a savage-looking creature with long teeth. What did it eat?"

My answer is, "Anything it wanted to." No, actually it is a total vegetarian! This is the same reasoning people employ when they look at a *Tyrannosaurus Rex's* mouth. They say, "Boy, he must have been a savage animal, ripping up other animals." On the other hand, if we take God at His Word, without our perceptions of what *we* think happened – if we just let God tell us in a straightforward way from Genesis –

we get a simple, yet profound, conclusion: All the animals were vegetarian!

Let me describe another example. In the Galapagos Islands, there is a marine iguana that is described as being very ferocious with sharp teeth and strong claws. However, it is a completely harmless vegetarian. Just because an animal has sharp teeth does not mean it is a meat eater. It just means that it has sharp teeth. There are many animals with sharp teeth even today that do not eat meat; for example, the panda, certain bears, and such like.

The History of the Universe

What I am saying is simply that we need to understand what the Bible is, first of all. The Bible is not just a book about salvation. The Bible is a revelation to us from the infinite Creator God. God has spoken to us in human language, which means we need to let the language of Scripture speak to us. If the Bible is a revelation from the infinite Creator, then it must be self-authenticating and self-attesting. We must let Scripture interpret Scripture. We cannot take fallible man's ideas and tell God what God means; we must let God tell us what He means.

I call the Bible "the history book of the universe." Christianity is not based in myth or some interesting stories. Christianity is based in real history. When you take the Bible from beginning to end, the following is that history:

In six days, God made everything – a perfect creation. Then the first man rebelled against God. That was the saddest day in the history of the universe. It changed everything, and death entered the world.

Following that, the wickedness of man became so great that God judged the world with a global flood. After that flood, there was an event called the Tower of Babel when God gave different languages, causing the population to split up and move to different places all over the Earth. This was the formation of different cultures.

Because of sin, man was cut off from God. So God sent His son to become one of us, to be of our blood, to be a man. The God-man had to die on a cross because death was the penalty for sin. He was raised from the dead so those who trust in Him can spend forever with Him. One day, there is going to be a perfect creation again when there will be no more sin, no more crying, no more death. It will be a new Heaven and a new Earth.

We need to understand this history and build our thinking upon it if we are going to understand the world today and provide solutions for the problems that we face. This is the true history of the universe.

Those major events of the past are a key to understanding who we are and what is wrong with our world. Understanding the major event – where Adam rebelled against God and sin entered the world, and death as a result – is *key* to understanding what has happened to this Earth.

Evolutionized. One of the problems we face is that because so many people have been indoctrinated to believe in millions of years, we do not understand the consequences of sin. In fact, I meet

In fact, I meet many Christians who blame God when a loved one dies. Actually, we should be getting angry at ourselves, at *our* sin. It is our sin that brought the judgment of death. We, in Adam, rebelled against God.

In fact, the Bible tells us that the whole of creation groans and travails in pain as it awaits the resurrection of the sons of God. Again, everything was affected by Adam's sin. Unless we really understand what that means and what its consequences are, we are not going to get it right when we start looking at the world. As Christians, we should be looking at the world through Biblical glasses and saying, "Ah – I know what happened in the past. I know what sin did. I know the origin of man. I know all these major events of history. I know why we are where we are today." When you look through those Biblical glasses, you have a foundation for applying the right way of thinking to what you see. That is what the Church has to get back to.

A Better Tack. Just a little sidebar here: Some people ask, "If you are saying there was no death before sin, how do you explain dinosaur fossils and other fossils all over the Earth?" I recommend that we take a better tack. If there had been a global flood, you would expect to find billions of dead things buried in rock layers laid down by water all over the Earth.

Interestingly, the evolutionist protests, "Where is the evidence for a global flood? All you find are billions of dead things buried in rock layers laid down by water all over the Earth."

The truth is that the fossil record is one of the greatest memorials that God left on this Earth. It is a testimonial to the flood as a judgment on this Earth. Now, I do not believe that all of this enormous fossil record came from the flood. Some of it came after the flood. But what we are looking at primarily is the graveyard of the flood crying out to the people of the world that man has rebelled against God, and that God has judged sin with death. It is a warning that He is going to judge next time by fire. Just as Noah had to go through the doorway of the ark to be saved, so we need to go through the doorway of the ark of the Lord Jesus Christ to be saved. That is the message of the fossil record. We are not seeing that message today, by and large, because people have the wrong glasses on.

Let us look a little more at this whole issue of death in depth because it is very, very important. I am going to talk about some of the pictures from one of our children's books, *A is for Adam*. (This is really a parents' book masquerading as a kid's book.) I have found that if you want to understand something, read the kids' books first!

We know that God made a tree, the tree of the knowledge of good and evil. Do you know what God said to Adam, the first man? "Adam, you can eat of all of the trees of the garden; but if you eat of this tree, you will surely die." This includes a Hebrew phrase which might be understood this way: "...dying, you will die. You will be dying; and you will die until you are dead."

Well what happened? Along came the devil in the form of a serpent, telling Eve, "You can eat the fruit."

Eve did and gave some to Adam, who ate also. I do not believe the fruit was an apple because the Bible does not say that. When Adam took the fruit, he rebelled against God. What do we call that? Sin.

What Is Sin?

Unless there was a literal serpent, a literal garden, a literal tree, literal fruit, a literal Adam, a literal temptation, and a literal fall, how can you define what sin is? That is what really blows my mind about people who say Genesis does not matter, that it is not important, that it could be myth. If Genesis is a myth, what does sin mean? Who defines sin? In the absence of Genesis, you can define sin any way you want to. Without Genesis, therefore, it is man who determines sin's meaning.

On the other hand, if this was a literal event in history, and it was a real man who was our ancestor, and he was the ancestor of all of us, then we, in Adam, sinned, and thus we are in rebellion against God. In short, the whole meaning of sin is tied up with its origin in Genesis.

When Adam and Eve sinned, they thought they could atone for their sins by making clothes and covering their nakedness; but, of course, you cannot atone for your sin so easily. What did God do? Genesis 3:21 gives us the answer, "Unto Adam and to his wife did the Lord God make coats of skins and clothed them." By the way, there we see the origin of clothing. Most people do not realize that the reason we wear clothes is because of Genesis.

If Genesis is not literal history, why not take your clothes off anytime you want? Of course, they are doing it more on TV these days and down on the beaches. The moral basis for clothing is right there in the book of Genesis. It means there are standards. God gave clothes because of sin. It is important to train our children that way.

If God made coats of skins, it means He must have killed at least one animal. Why did He do that? According to Hebrews 9:22, "Without shedding of blood, is no remission of sins." My favorite illustration in *A Is for Adam* is the one where Adam and Eve are clothed in lamb's wool clothing. We show the slain lamb and the blood from the lamb. (Illustration on preceding page used by permission of Answers in Genesis.)

The Bible does not say it was a lamb, but I really believe it was a lamb because this is the first blood sacrifice as a covering for sin – a picture of what was to come in Jesus Christ, the Lamb of God that takes away the sin of the world. What we have here is a picture of the Gospel message right there in Genesis. Of course, the blood of animals cannot take away our sin. We are not connected to the animal kingdom. It had to be a man, a perfect man. This is why God sent His Son to become one of us. If this event is not literal history, why believe the Gospel?

Genesis 3:15 says, "I will put enmity between thee and the woman, between thy seed and her seed, it shall bruise thy head, but thou shalt bruise His heel." That is the Gospel message in Genesis again! But if Genesis is not real, if that story is an allegory, then the Gospel must be an allegory. If the first Adam is an allegory, then by all logic, so is the last Adam, who is Jesus Christ. This is another illustration of how important it is to believe in a literal Genesis. The whole meaning of death is tied up with its origin in Genesis – death because of sin. That is why we see a groaning world all around us. In fact, foundational to understanding the Gospel is the fact that Jesus Christ created all things, that sin entered into the world and death as a result. It is the reason that Jesus Christ, the Son of God, became a man to suffer death on a cross and to be raised from the dead. It all hangs together, does it not?

But do you know the sad thing? So many Christians today believe in millions of years of Earth history or some form of evolution. When God brought Eve to Adam in the garden, she said, "Oh, Adam, this is such a perfect world."

"Yes, Eve, it is very good, just as God said," Adam agreed.

However, if the garden is sitting on billions of bones (dead things), bloodshed, disease, and suffering, you wipe out the message of the cross. You destroy the basis of the atonement. It blows my mind – the number of Christians, Christian leaders, and theologians – who say, "You can believe in millions of years of the Earth's development; it does not matter." Oh yes it does! What you are doing is taking fallible man's dating methods, adding them to the Bible, and re-interpreting the Bible. If we take God's Word alone, would you ever get the idea of millions of years of death, disease, and bloodshed before sin? Absolutely not.

When evolutionists look at bones of dinosaurs and so on, they see examples of infections, arthritis, cancer, osteomyelitic infection, abscesses, and all sorts of interesting things. The fossil record is full of disease. Did God pronounce everything good when there was all this disease, suffering, and bloodshed?

I received an interesting call from a pastor's wife who complained, "We cannot come to your seminar because you insist in believing in a literal Genesis. Genesis is not important; it does not matter. It could be myth; it is not essential. Why can't we just all as Christians get together and agree on the essentials?"

I asked, "What do you mean by 'the essentials'?"

"That Jesus Christ died on a cross and was raised from the dead."

I followed up with, "May I ask you a question? Why did Jesus die for our sins? What is sin?"

She said, "Well, rebellion."

I said, "How do you know that? Is that your opinion or somebody else's? How do you know what is rebellion? I know some preachers who teach that sin is a lack of self-esteem. I mean, what is sin?"

She said, "Sin is rebellion."

"How do you know that?"

She said, "I know what you are trying to do."

"Yes, I know what I am trying to do. Let me ask you a question. Is it essential ultimately to believe in original sin?"

"Absolutely."

"Think about it," I said, referring her to 1 Corinthians 15:45, Jesus Christ is called the last Adam. Then I mentioned 1 Corinthians 15:22, where we are told that "as in Adam, all die, even so in Christ shall all be made alive." 1 Corinthians 15:45 also talks about the first Adam.

Then I asked her, "Thinking about the first Adam and the last Adam, you tell me, which Adam is nonessential to the Gospel? They are both absolutely essential, are they not? You cannot understand the Gospel or explain it if you do not understand that the first Adam, of whom we are all descendants, rebelled against God. Sin came into the world, and death as a result. That is why Jesus Christ (called the last Adam) became one of us to take the first Adam's place, to be the new head. All people are of Adam's race – there is only one race of humans.

What has happened, however, is evolutionary teaching has indoctrinated us in the idea that there are different races of people that evolved at different times. Sadly, because of this indoctrination, many of us do not really have a correct understanding of humanity. In fact, our minds have been clouded. Darwin forever changed things back in 1859 when he popularized the idea of different races evolving at different times. In fact, regardless of what people say, the teaching of evolution in public schools, even today, is inherently a racist philosophy. It is about time we woke up to that fact. Darwinism teaches that there are different cultures that evolved at different times; and some are more closely related to their apelike ancestors than others.

One Race

From a Biblical perspective, we all go back to one man and one woman. We are ALL descendants of Adam and Eve. In fact, biologically speaking, there is only one race, anyway; there are not different races. Even the evolutionists know that.

Speaking before the 1995 American Association for the Advancement of Science convention in Atlanta, C. Loring Brace, a University of Michigan biological anthropologist, said, "Race is a social construct derived mainly from perceptions conditioned by events of recorded history, and it has no basic biological reality." When you think about it, evolutionists – in fact, all secular scientists – say that all human beings are *Homo sapiens*. We are all the same genus, species, and subspecies because we are all related, because we all go back to one man and one woman. That is why we are all *Homo sapiens*. Do you know what the Bible really says? It says that we are all one blood (Acts 17). That is one of the ways I like to put it. We all go back to Adam and Eve.

One of the problems we have is this. Too many people in our churches and in the secular world say, "But look at the differences." There are differences in skin color, in eye shape, and in nose shapes, for instance. People think these differences must have developed over a long period of time. They think that these differences are major. Because of this evolutionary indoctrination, we tend to think in terms of long time periods. So we do not really understand our history.

The truth is: the genetic differences between the cultures of the world are insignificant!!! This is very important. Once we understand our history based upon the Bible, what a difference that makes in the way we approach everything.

Cain's Wife. The most common question I am asked is, Where did Cain get his wife? One minister told me he never could answer the question. He just asked people, "What are you interested in somebody else's wife for?" That is not a very good answer, is it? We need to be able to answer the question. By the way, do *you* know why it is an important question? If you cannot answer it, how do YOU defend the notion that we all go back to one man and one woman?

The other thing we have to account for is this: what about these differences we see among all the cultures of the world? Let us start from the Bible. Again, 1 Corinthians 15:45 refers to "the first man Adam." How many men were there to start with? *One.* Genesis 3:20 says, "And Eve was to be the mother of ALL living." How many women were there to start with? The answer is *one.*

In fact, recall that Acts 17:26 points out that "God hath made of one blood" all nations of men who would dwell on the face of the Earth. In other words, Paul says that we all came from one man. Genesis 5:4 provides a summary concerning Adam's life: "And he begat sons and ... daughters." Now, since there were no other people on the Earth, brothers must have married sisters!

Some will stutter, "But, but, but, but, but..." But what? "But you are not allowed to do that today." I will have to agree; that is true. Do you know why? The law against close intermarriage did not come until the time of Moses (Leviticus 18).

Genetically Speaking. This is another example of why we need to understand our history. The basic problem is this – sin affected everything, including our genes. The Bible record indicates that Adam and Eve lived about 6,000 years ago. Consequently, we have suffered from 6,000 years of the curse. Interesting things have happened over that time. Have you ever heard of *mutations*? These are changes in our genes – in a word, "mistakes." There are thousands of them. We each have literally hundreds of mistakes in our genes. In fact, we are getting worse, not better, every day.

People get one set of genes from the father and one from the mother. Since close relatives are more likely to have the same set of genetic mistakes, if brother and sister were to marry and those mistakes got together, you would be more likely to have problems in the offspring. You would be more likely to get some sort of deformity. Therefore, it is better to marry someone further away in relationship. Of course, then you collect different mistakes. So we continue to deteriorate anyway.

As we go back in history toward Adam and Eve, would you expect fewer mistakes or more mistakes? Fewer, of course. Keep going back until you are before sin entered the world. How many mistakes would you encounter in Adam and Eve? Zero. Adam and Eve's children would have had relatively few mistakes as well.

Before sin entered our universe, God's plan was for one man and one woman to marry for life. That is what marriage is all about. So I ask again, was there any problem with brother and sister marriage originally? No.

That is why I asked the question, "Can you marry your relative?" The truth is that when you get married you HAVE to marry your relative! We are all related to each other, whether we like it or not. That is why when people say to me, "I am praying for my relatives," I ask if they are praying for all six billion of them!

So, originally, brother and sister married. Some ask, "Isn't that incest?" No. Incest is a modern word that applies to today's situation. When the relationship is one man for one woman for life, that is what marriage is all about. We do not marry a close relative today because of the very real probability of compounding genetic mistakes.

For the sake of convenience, I am going to talk about racial groups and races even though I believe that there is but one race. The main racial groups that scientists divide cultures into are Caucasoid, Mongoloid, Negroid, and Australoid. People ask, "How does one explain the major differences if we all go back to one man and one woman?" The truth is that there are not major differences. In order to clarify this point, consider the following review of basic genetics.

We have DNA in our cells, the "blueprint" of all the information that builds us. These are chemicals lined up in an order that is sort of like a code, if you like.

Can you imagine putting beads and dashes along a piece of rope to spell out help? In fact, you could write the entire Bible in Morse code. In a sense, there are "marks" like beads and dashes, if you will, on our DNA. We get one set of genes from our father and one from our mother. In fact, I want you to look at it this way: (Illustration on next page used by permission of Answers in Genesis.)

Here is a male and a female, and here are some pairs of genes, Aa Bb Cc. "A" male and "a" female each have those. By the way, if we were to take any one man and any one woman from among those of you reading this book, there is enough information in your genes such that (if it were physically possible), you could actually have more children than atoms in the known universe and still not get two who look the same. That is how much variability there is in our DNA. So you see, from just two people, there are billions and billions of possible unique combinations.

If we look at just the first three genes, we could end up with AA, BB, CC, or aa, bb, cc, and so forth. This is the *opposite* of evolution. For evolution to occur, you have to *add* new information. In reality, natural selection often results in a loss of information.

MALE
Aa Bb Cc   x

FEMALE
Aa Bb Cc

Possible information in egg/sperm cells:

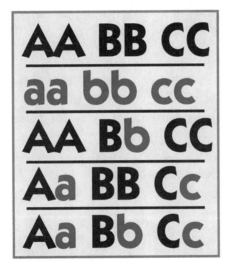

Possible combinations in offspring:

AA BB CC
aa bb cc
AA Bb CC
Aa BB Cc
Aa Bb Cc

Each of us has a different combination of information. Some of us have information for black hair; some for brown hair; and so on.

To give you an example, suppose two dogs came off Noah's ark. They got "married" and had children. Their children married and had children. You could eventually end up – as they split up the gene pool and went to different places across the Earth – with wolf, dingo, coyote, African wild dog, and on and on. That is not evolution. Biologists call that specialization by natural selection. All that happened was, the information was split up and sent different combinations in different directions. Because they did not mix together anymore, we have these different varieties.

It is very similar with humans. Take the issue of skin color. Most do not realize that all of us basically have the same skin color. We all have a pigment called *melanin*. One can have a lot of it and be very dark. One can have a little bit and be very light. One can be anywhere in between. It is not a matter of different color; it is a matter of how much or how little you have. I do not have a lot of melanin, to be honest. The majority of the world's population is middle-brown, much darker than I am. In our illustration, assume there are two genes for skin color, A and B, and their corresponding a and b, if one has all big As and big Bs, that could mean lots of melanin (very dark). Lower case a and b produce a little bit of melanin (very light). With a mixture of AaBb, you would be in the middle (middle-brown). It would make sense that Adam and Eve would have been in the middle.

Even though there are more genes than this, the principle is the same. If Adam and Eve had been in the middle (<u>Aa</u> <u>Bb</u>), their children could have been dark to light in one generation. There are families like that today. You can see that very clearly in India, for instance. You see it in America, too. In fact, I have an interesting picture from Britain captioned "Britain's Amazing Twins." One is very dark, almost black, and the other one is very light. Obviously, they are not identical twins.

But how could that variation be? Very simple. For instance, if you have a certain combination of genes in a very dark wife and a fairly light father, one of the children could end up with a combination for not much melanin and the other could end up with a combination of a lot of melanin. This is very, very easy to understand.

A common question I receive is, "How is it that some cultures only produce black people, some only produce light people, and so on?" Think about it like this. How do we get our different varieties of dogs like our poodles, dachshunds, retrievers, pit bulls, and the like? We have bred most of them in the last few hundred years, really. We look for certain characteristics that we want. We only breed animals with those characteristics, and we separate them from the others. And how do you keep a poodle a poodle? You do not let it breed with a Great Dane or anything else.

What event could have happened in history to cause the human population to split up and distribute different combinations of genes in different directions? The Tower of Babel, of course, is the epochal event when God gave different languages, causing people to split up and go to different places all over the Earth. Now, depending on who married whom and who died out for whatever reason, if you eventually ended up with all people in a group having AAbb, they could never produce light again, only dark, unless they mixed back in with the others.

If you had some that only ended up with a and b, they could only produce light, never dark. If you had a group where all ended up with Aabb, then they could only produce middle brown children.

These things are very, very easy to understand. When we look at matters like the variation in skin color, that is a major issue simply because most people *look* at *it* as a big problem, which it is not.

Social Darwinism

This leads us to an important fact. If you take the so-called Caucasoid race, the genetic variation between any two individuals has been calculated to be only 0.2 percent – less than 1 percent. If you take the so-called Negroid race, the genetic variation between any two individuals is also 0.2 percent. On the other hand, the so-called "racial differences" (skin "color," eye shape, etc.) constitute only 0.012 percent genetic difference. It is insignificant; the difference between the races is only about half the variation within the races. In either case, the differences are so minor, they are negligible. That is why I prefer the term "people group" instead of race.

The major reason people think the variations are major is because back in 1859 something changed our way of thinking. When he published *The Origin of Species by Means of Natural Selection or the Preservation of Favoured Races in the Struggle for Life*, Darwin promoted a racist philosophy that forever changed many people's thinking. At that time, "race" to the English race, the Irish race, and so on. Today, when people think of race, many have been so indoctrinated by evolutionary thinking that there is some prejudice there. Darwin said that certain cultures like the Negroid and the Australoid were closer to the apes than others. In fact, the Australian Aborigines were considered the "missing link." They were hunted down like animals in Australia; and 10,000 "specimens" were sent to museums around the world in the name of evolution.

Others have been quick to piggyback on the concept of "favoured races." Darwin's "bulldog" in Germany, Ernst Haeckel, said in his book, *The History of Creation*:

> In order to be convinced of this important result, it is above all things necessary to study and compare the mental life of wild savages and of children. At the lowest stage of human mental development are the Australians [I hope he is not talking about me], some tribes of the Polynesians, and the Bushmen, Hottentots, some of the Negro tribes. (page 362)

Can you imagine this being taught in universities? History bears testimony to how this kind of teaching permeated people's thinking even to the end of the 20th century. In fact, Haeckel goes on to say,

> Nothing, however, is perhaps more remarkable in

this respect than that some of the wildest tribes in southern Asia and eastern Africa have no trace whatever of the first foundations of all human civilization, of family life, and marriage. They live together in herds like apes, generally climbing on trees and eating fruits; they do not know of fire, and use stones and clubs as weapons, just like the higher apes. (page 363)

Even though there were racist attitudes before Darwin, you cannot get much more racist than that.

The sad thing is that there always will be racist attitudes when you do not have a right Biblical foundation. There were people who believed in the Greek idea of the "great chain of being." They expected to find men with monkeys' tails and all that sort of thing. Racist attitudes existed before Darwin and for many reasons.

There is no doubt that Darwinian evolution fueled racism. Today, textbooks continue to perpetuate such myths. A typical book from a public school today shows the supposed development of ape-like creatures and so on through humans. This espouses a racist philosophy – that certain cultures are more closely connected to the apes than others.

In short, evolution is inherently a racist philosophy. One of the main problems we have today is that there is a hangover which permeates our entire culture. There is a prejudice, particularly when it comes to skin color, because we have been so indoctrinated in evolutionary philosophy that we are looking at the world through the wrong glasses. It is about time we put on our Biblical glasses. It is sad that many churches teach that you can believe in evolution and add God to it. No wonder we have race problems! No wonder we have racist attitudes!

There is another problem in our churches. Dr. Hugh Rass, a leader of the Progressive Creation Movement, said in his children's book,

> Starting two to four millions years ago, God began creating man-like mammals.... These creatures stood on two feet, had large brains, and used tools. Some even buried their dead and painted on cave walls. They were very different from us. They had no spirit. They did not have a conscience like we do. They did not worship God or establish religious practices. In time, all of these manlike creatures went extinct. Then 10,000 to 25,000 years ago, God replaced them with Adam and Eve.

When teaching like this permeates our church, there is no wonder we have problems – especially when this particular "Christian" leader accepts methods that date the Aborigines back to 40,000 or 60,000 years. Are the Aborigines not descendants of Adam and Eve? No wonder we have massive problems in the church concerning racial issues.

This may sound simplistic to some. To me it is not. We should just take God at His Word that we all:

> ➢ Go back to Adam and Eve.

> ➢ Have a problem called sin.

> ➢ Need the solution of Jesus Christ.

> ➢ Need to build our thinking on the Word of God, and not take our prejudices to the Bible, reinterpreting God's Word on the basis of man's opinion.

Interracial Marriage

When I say that, some people wonder, "What about interracial marriage?" Let me quickly go through the way I teach my children about so-called "interracial" marriage. I tell them there is no such thing as interracial marriage because from a biological perspective there is only one race. I teach them that we need to work from the Bible. The logical place to begin is by determining the primary purposes of marriage. One of the primary purposes is stated in Malachi 2 – to produce godly offspring. How do you produce godly offspring? In Ephesians 5 and Matthew 19, we are told that a married couple becomes one. You become one because you are one flesh.

We are told in 2 Corinthians not to be unequally yoked with an unbeliever. I teach my children not to date a non-Christian. Their mate is to be a Christian, and they are to build their marriage on the Bible.

Next, they need to understand that if they do marry someone from a very different culture, that person will think differently from my child. Even though the person is Christian and the two are one in Christ, there can be some problems in communication. Two people considering marriage need to understand up front that if they grew up in totally different cultures there will likely be communication problems. Marriages have failed because of this. Next, we need to understand that in some cultures, there is a stigma on certain mixes. The stigma is wrong, of course; but that is the way it is. People need to be prepared for that before they approach marriage.

We also need to understand Biblical patterns. For example, Rahab, a Canaanite, and Ruth, a Moabite, trusted the one true God of the Israelites. The genealogy of Jesus (Matthew 1) documents that Ruth was in the lineage of Christ. Most scholars agree that Rahab was in the lineage of Christ, too. The issue there was that they trusted the one true God. Think about it! Rahab, a descendant of Ham, married a descendant of Shem – leading to Christ.

Some point to Acts 17:26 where it says that God

... made of one blood all nations of men to dwell on all the face of the Earth, and determined the times before appointed, and the bounds of their habitation.

They interpret that passage to mean that God did not want people to mix across the Earth. That verse has nothing to do with marriage. It is talking about God's raising up nations and destroying kingdoms. These matters are totally in His control. That passage is much clearer when we understand it in context.

You see, we really ARE of one blood. We are ALL equal before God. We ALL go back to Adam and Eve. The differences are minor. When we understand the true Biblical history and have a firm foundation from a literal Genesis, it becomes so simple to apply that thinking to everything we encounter in the world.

We have to understand that sin has distorted our understanding through the way we have been indoctrinated. Our education system plays a major role in this distortion.

One last thing: if there is Adam in your ancestry, that means God made you, and God sets the rules. To the contrary, if you believe there is ape in your ancestry, then who owns you? You do. Who sets the rules? You do.

When we start with God's Word, we know that there was one Adam and, therefore, one race. We know that marriage means one man for one woman for life. We know why we wear clothes. We know the rightful place for sex. We have a consistent, logical worldview because we have a foundation.

On the other hand, if you start with one of the popular notions, such as a belief that man can determine truth (that is what evolution is really all about), why not do what you want with sex? Why not abort babies? Why not treat cultures the way you want? It is up to you to determine who is your equal. So why not have racist attitudes?

What is happening in our culture today is the collapse of the Christian fabric and an increase in humanistic philosophy. The reason is quite simple. We have gotten away from the foundation of the authority of the Word of God. We have said that man determines truth. One of the sad things is that in the past – even when America was basically a Christian nation and had the foundation of the authority of the Word of God – we still had prejudices and all sorts of biases because we had been indoctrinated by humanistic, evolutionary philosophy. The remedy for these ills is to get back to the authority of the Word.

I sum it up with two castles: The foundation of the first castle is evolution. The structure is humanism. Issues like abortion and racism come out of that. (Used by permission of Answers in Genesis.)

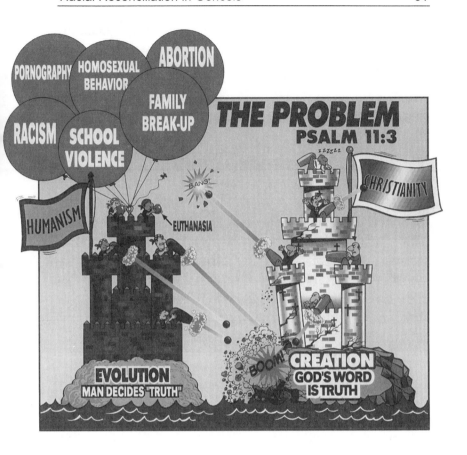

(Used by permission of Answers in Genesis.)

The foundation of the first castle is evolution. The structure is humanism. Issues like abortion and racism come out of that. The humanists know that if they can knock out the foundation of the authority of the Word of God the structure of Christianity will collapse.

They take potshots at the issues. The problem is that we fall away from the foundational truths of the Bible. We swallow the humanistic lie that man determines truth.

The foundation of the second castle is creation, which includes God's Word, truth, and the structure of Christianity.

The humanists are very clever. They know that if they can knock out the foundation of the authority of the Word of God the structure of Christianity will collapse. Do you know where they start? With Genesis 1-11, of course. Once you knock out Genesis 1-11, you knock out the rest of the Bible.

What do Christians do? They shoot each other. They shoot into nowhere. They take potshots at the issues. A lot of people today fight racism and abortion, but abortion and racism are not the problems. They are *symptoms*. The real problem is that we have gotten away from the foundational truths of the Bible. We have swallowed the humanistic lie that man can determine truth.

The solution to it all is very simple. (Illustration used by permission of Answers in Genesis.)

We need to begin by restoring the authority of the Word of God and knocking out that wrong foundation – the foundation that people can determine truth for themselves.

If the foregoing discussion has interested you, our organization has an incredible web site called: www.AnswersInGenesis.org On our website, you can download many pages of resource material. We also have a colorful magazine, *Creation*. It goes to more than a hundred countries to teach people how to defend God's Word in today's culture.

(Illustration used by permission of Answers in Genesis.)

The foundation of the second castle is creation, which includes God's Word, truth, and the structure of Christianity. Christians today fight racism and abortion, *symptoms* of the problems.

The solution is to restore the authority of the Word of God and knock out that wrong foundation — the foundation that people can determine truth for themselves.

One of the problems in the church is that many Christians do not know how to defend God's Word. A subscription to *Creation* helps you deal with the issues of today at a foundational level.

In addition, we have a book that deals with the issues of the origin of races in much, much more detail, *The Answers Book*. It also talks about the Gap Theory and carbon dating, about the days of Creation, Cain's wife, and dinosaurs. Another book, *The Lie*, deals with how Christians need to believe Genesis 1-11 and how an understanding of Genesis 1-11 is prerequisite to understanding Christianity, the rest of the Bible, how to defend our faith, and a true Christian worldview.

When it comes to talking about racial reconciliation, about who we are, about where we originated, and about the problems of our culture – first of all, what we need to understand as Christians is that we need to be out there preaching the authority of the Word of God. You cannot change a nation from the top down when it deteriorated from the foundation up. To deal with those issues, you need to deal with foundations. If people are going to change their attitudes regarding other cultures and each other, they need to understand that they are sinners. They need to understand that they are descendants of Adam and Eve. They need to understand the holiness of God – that sin brought judgment. They need to understand that they need to fall on their knees before a holy God and come to the Lord Jesus Christ in faith and repentance, trusting Him as Lord and Savior. They need to build their thinking on the Word of God and have a consistent

Christian worldview. Christians need to get out there and be salt in the culture.

If we are going to change this culture, we need to preach the Word of God authoritatively. That is what it is all about, and that is the message that I want to leave with you.

4 – Deep and Meaningful Cross-Cultural Relationships

A Conversation for Committing to Reconciliation

Ray Hilbert and Ken Johnson[1]

[Editors' note: This chapter developed from a conversational workshop facilitated by Ray Hilbert and Ken Johnson.]

Ken Johnson: I have some startling news for you. "Race" relations are in a sorry state in this country, in case you hadn't noticed. This is bad both for individuals and for our society as a whole. But that's not all. Worse yet, the race problem among Christians has a negative impact on

---

[1] Ken Johnson is a nationally known high school assembly speaker, evangelist, and recording artist. Ray Hilbert is the Promise Keepers' North Central Regional Director. Together they are co-founders of Reconcilors of Christ, a Christ-centered ministry dedicated to demonstrating a practical, hands-on approach to racial reconciliation through workshops and training seminars in order to facilitate true reconciliation in the body of Christ and in society.

Ken is also founder of Helping Hand Group, a ministry partnering with schools, churches, men's groups, and special groups to spread the message of Christ. In addition, Ray is co-founder of a church and food pantry focusing on serving the needs of inner-city people.

the credibility of the Gospel. As Christians, we need to commit ourselves before God that this will not continue to be true. Further, with God as our source and strength, we should commit ourselves to being part of the solution, since anyone who is not part of the solution is part of the problem.

This is such an obvious conclusion that I am amazed I did not think of it years ago. As it stands, it was not until I met Ray Hilbert that I began to see how Satan has manipulated the race thing to hinder the witness of the Church of Jesus Christ. This chapter will explore some of the dynamics Ray and I have experienced as we have attempted to flesh out the Gospel right where we live.

Ray and I are from totally different cultures and backgrounds. Ray is the most organized guy I know. On the other hand, I am probably the most unorganized guy that you will ever meet. Perhaps that is why God put us together. It is amazing how opposites seem to attract. What really unite us together are our love for and acceptance of a mighty Savior. God has used these ingredients to intertwine our lives together, hopefully to model for people who examine our lives that they can get past this skin thing, too. I have a T-shirt that says, "It's not a black thing. It's not a white thing. It's a Jesus thing." On the back it concludes, "Enough said."

Biblical Reconciliation

We are taught in the Scriptures that we have been reconciled to the cross. A Christian's relationship with Christ is secure. In the area of interpersonal relationships, however, reconciliation is still needed. The

Church has not done many of the things that it needs to do to bring about reconciliation so that more successful examples can develop within the Church.

Ray Hilbert and I have made a commitment to the search for Biblical truth. We are determined to pursue this quest even if it means denying where we come from and who we think we are or should be. In addition, we have intentionally looked at what we have to do to break down the walls that separate people of different colors. We have made a conscious decision that we have to identify those things that are barriers to reconciliation. Then we have to do our part to *intentionally* knock down the barriers.

While many say they are committed to reconciliation, in most cases they are not intentional. Ray joined a church, not because it was an African American church, but because they were teaching the Word. It is a tremendous church. They love God. Ray is intentionally saying, "I am not going to be affected simply because there are not a lot of white folks there."

I have intentionally joined a predominantly white church. Not because it is a white church, but because they teach the Word. My spirit bears witness with their spirit, and my kids love it there. We have intentionally said we are not going to let those traditional barriers of where we have come from stop what God has called us to do. This chapter is a combination of what our will says and what God's Word says. We subject ourselves to His Word and to bringing our will into subjection to Him.

Ray Hilbert: God has taught us to be sensitive to different personalities and different cultures. Ken has already touched on the fact that I am highly organized. If something is not in its place, I get nervous. Being late to me is being less than 20 minutes early. Ken is more laid back. He seems to say, "We'll get there when we get there." Similarly, I know that there are different personalities and different cultures represented by the readers of this book. We hope to lay out principles which will work with a variety of personalities and cultural identifications. Some of what we have found to work may need to be adapted to fit your particular personality or local setting.

Reconciliation demands coming together in our common poverty, our obvious weaknesses, and our otherwise inexcusable sin in order to receive God's riches, strength, and grace. Poverty refers to more than economics. Poverty also describes a spiritual state of being. Every one of us is a sinner. That is the ultimate poverty before an almighty and holy God. Consequently, the foundation on which to begin to build relationships is understanding that we have some things in common.

Ken comes from a different cultural experience, economic background, and spiritual journey than I. But we realized very early on that if it were not for Jesus Christ and His saving grace, we would both be lost. The government can spend billions of dollars, and every social agency that wants to can try to implement every well-intentioned program. The Equal Employment Opportunity Commission can try to do everything they want to do to equal things out. These goals cannot be met, however, until we get to the heart issue – that we are all sinners, and we all have that common poverty.

Ken: That is, we must not ever allow the culture of individuals to be the reference by which we build or refuse to build relationships. If we allow that, we lose the common ground that is so necessary. My not having a dad in the home, my mom being a prostitute, and my uncle being a dope dealer and a heroin addict – all of those things are insignificant under the blood.

On the other hand, Ray's dad was an alcoholic and was abusive to his mom. Ray grew up without positive role models until another man came into his life and helped him with baseball. None of those things are significant enough to serve as barriers to fellowship. Even though I had a relationship with a brother who had millions of dollars, I was still a sinner. Our starting point is not where we come from. Rather, it is a matter of to whom we now belong. For Christians, that's Jesus Christ. That is why we cannot ever allow where we came from to determine where we are going.

Ray: Some specific examples of how God has used our relationship both in the Body and publicly may help clarify the point we are making. To start with, God is changing me. I used to be a slave to a stick-to-the-outline mentality. I now hear God saying, "Share your heart." When Ken called me for some last-minute dialogue on our recent workshop, I did not freak out as I might have several years ago. Instead, I have learned to ask, "What's up with this, God?"

Three Measurable Levels of Relationship

We all go through three levels of relationship.

Acquaintance Level. The first level is where we are simply acquaintances, where we talk about things like:

"Hey, did you see the Pacer game last night?"

"Wow, this sure is great weather we are having."

An acquaintance is a person who knows you only slightly. Her or his knowledge of you is not intimate. We all have acquaintances. All relationships should begin here. Most of our relationships will remain at this level.

When we consult with clients in organizations, we like to help them understand this dimension of relationships. Our work is quite interesting, particularly in churches where people think they are really close. We help them to see that, contrary to their impressions, many of their relationships are nothing more than acquaintances. We have them hold up one hand and we say, "If you are sitting next to a person whose first name you know, keep your hand up." We instruct them to keep their hands up as long as they can answer a stream of questions: "What is the person's last name? Their spouse's name? How many children do they have?" Pretty soon, most of those hands start dropping because – even in our good churches – many people are still at the acquaintance level. Their knowledge of each other is less intimate than they think.

Friendship Level. Level two involves being friends. A friend is a person who knows, likes, and trusts you – a person who shares your sorrows and joys. That goes beyond the weather, beyond "I sure am sorry to hear about the death of your uncle." A friend is someone who is concerned about your well being in body, soul, and spirit. Proverbs says that a friend loves at all times. In fact, Proverbs also says, "A wound from a friend is better than a kiss from an enemy."

Brother/Sister Level. Some relationships progress to a third level, that of being a brother. A friend is great to have; but the Bible tells us that "a brother is born for adversity."

This is where it really starts getting deep. A brother is a person who recognizes and shares your spiritual parentage – someone who cries when you cry and rejoices when you are joyful. Brothers have the same father. We have an automatic bond, which may need to be cultivated. In addition, this suggests that – in the deepest spiritual sense – it is impossible to be a brother or a sister to someone who is not a Christian.

Ken: That is the reason we are here. If God is our Father and we are brothers and sisters in the Lord, that settles it. We have all been adopted into the King's family. We are all princes and princesses of a mighty King. As a result, we must live according to our heavenly Father's rules and mandates – not by our earthly fathers' dictates any longer. That is why our lineage of spirituality runs deeper than our cultural lineage. There lies the beginning of who we all are anyway.

We are all related because we all come from the same two persons. So, it all comes back to that anyway. That is why Ray, as a Caucasian who has a small amount of melanin (pigmentation; see Ham's chapter), is more my brother than someone who may have more melanin, even though I may share a commonality in pigmentation with the latter. What unites us together is not the hue of our skin. It is our relationship with our Savior and with our true Daddy.

Ray: Do you know why you have brothers and sisters? It was based on the activity of the father.

Ken: Momma had a little bit to do with it, too.

Ray: So when you look at it from a spiritual perspective, brotherhood and sisterhood are based not on what we have done, but on the activity of our parents. We do not have a choice in the matter. Similarly, reconciliation is not a choice. Other chapters in this book explore how reconciliation is a Biblical mandate.

How to Begin Reconciliation

Step one in reconciliation is starting the process. The foundation is prayer. A prayer foundation is a must to establish the necessary commitment for cross-cultural and cross-denominational relationships. Joint prayer will reconcile us to God and to each other. This is an excellent strategy. It is a Biblical requirement in any relationship. I have found that it is impossible to hold anger when we are in prayer together. God will not allow it. There is an incredible thing that comes over you when you go to prayer with somebody. As we try to develop cross-cultural relationships with someone, there might be some animosity or some discouragement. Prayer with that person is the most important and most effective strategy we can ever use.

Ken: I pray feverishly – about an hour every morning. I pray for every pastor who has ever been associated with any person with whom I have come into contact. I pray for every pastor who has ever been associated with any person with whom I have had a meaningful relationship. I pray for Ray, specifically for things that he has asked me to pray for as well as for things that I discern about him. Prayer creates a tremendous bond. If you do not like something specific about your pastor, start praying for him. Then what may happen is, your outlook and your attitude may begin to change. Prayer is something that we do not often allocate enough time to because we are in so much of a hurry.

As a practical matter, since I spend a lot of time in my car, I have begun to turn the radio off and devote my driving time to prayer. This way I fill a lot of time with doing something meaningful. This helps me to rejoice and reflect on the things for which I am thankful.

Ray: Be intentional about reaching out to people. Ask not only how you may pray *for* them but also how you may pray *with* them. Engage them in the process. God has promised to be responsible for the results. He will change the hearts. Our responsibility is to pray.

Ken and I did not enter into our friendship because we were trying to develop a cross-cultural relationship. We began because each of us was looking for accountability in our lives. God has developed it into something even greater than we could ask or think.

Facilitate Relationship Building. By the way, I think our nomenclature is something of an oxymoron. (An oxymoron is a combination of two words that are contradictory. The most common humorous example is *military intelligence*.) To suggest that there is a step-by-step process to reconciliation is an oxymoron. Reconciliation is more than a process. It is a lifelong journey. However, for the purpose of giving bite-size directions and to help you get your mind around the concept, we have split it into steps.

A very important logistical consideration involves selecting a meeting place that is comfortable for all involved. Time spent together should be used to build trust. Communicate your heart to discover issues about your relationship that may be below the surface.

Too many times we try (and particularly the Anglo community is incredibly guilty of this) to invite other cultures to come to our church, to this, to that, and to the other function. That is great; but how many times do we go into their environment?

Ken: This is an extremely critical point. Some may wonder how you get others to come to your functions. Kids do not have to go looking for dope dealers in their communities. Bad influences make themselves accessible. So where in the world are the good Christian influences?

Jesus said "GO" into the world. He did not say *pray* that you go, *strategize* that you go, or *find the right philosophy* when you go. He said, "GO." By going, you begin the process. Some African American families, especially the impoverished ones, may feel intimidated at coming into white communities. At the same time, you may be thinking, "They're coming to a lovely home with wonderful, gracious hosts. They'll enjoy the experience."

You should go into *their* comfort zone, too – right where they live. Venture out into areas where you feel uncomfortable, areas where you might have to wonder, "Man, what are people going to do to my car?" When you go to their turf; they will show you around. That is the best way you can find a mutual relationship.

It would have been a radical change for most suburban Christians to visit the neighborhood where I grew up. Ray has taken advantage of many opportunities to go places where we both have had to watch not only our cars, but also our backs. But we still go intentionally. We encourage you to work at intentionally developing a relationship with someone interested, not only in holding you accountable, but also in relating to you right where you are and vicè versà.

Ray: God is reversing our mentality. We have always talked about the suburbs going into the inner city. I have seen more and more inner-city ministries reaching out into the suburbs. We all know about the down-and-outers. There are also the up-and-outers. If those people could be reached for Christ, think of all the resources in time, talent, and treasure that would become available to advance the Kingdom of God.

I happen to belong to Eastern Star Baptist Church. One of the awesome things that our church did was to have a contingency of the membership sign a covenant that we would attend a church plant on Sunday mornings out in the white suburbs in an elementary school a mile and a half from my house. Our initial six-month commitment has been extended several times, adding up to four years now.

There are 600 people or so who attend the Sunday morning service. There are probably less than 20 who are not black. My neighbors have asked me, "What are all those black people doing down there at the elementary school?" It gives me a great opportunity to say *WE* are having church. The neat part about this is there is a new perception of what God is doing now. This interracial worship experience is removing the cultural stripe from the neighbors' perception of worship by the people of God. This is happening because we are obeying a Biblical mandate. That is a great example to the community.

Promise Keepers sponsored a project in Indianapolis recently called "Serve the City." We brought together a number of suburban churches and partnered them with inner-city churches to work on the facilities at some of those inner-city places of worship.

Let me tell you a quick story about what happened as a result of one of these partnerships. A white lady from one of the suburban churches developed a great relationship with one of the black children, a little girl of about five years of age. After they got to know each other, the lady would hug the little girl and just spend time with her. The little girl went home to her mother one day and asked, "Momma, how come you never hug me like that white lady does?" That mother subsequently came to the church and has now gotten saved and is involved in the ministry of the church simply because somebody went and loved on her daughter and did not just come in and bring stuff. They came in and spent time and invested their lives. Isn't that the model of Christ's love?

What's a Guy to Do? So, what do you do when two congregations get together? Share your common spiritual experiences. But keep my mom's saying in mind, "Some people are so heavenly minded, they are no earthly good." True, you need to experience and share the spiritual journey together; but you also need to share some human experiences. I do not care what people's cultures are or what their economic backgrounds are – the same things are important: love, respect, honor, courtesy, and the like.

Listing all the things you have in common is a great strategy. An exercise we do in one of our workshops with ethnically diverse groups involves sending all of the African Americans with Ken to one room. I take the Anglos to another room. In our groups, we start listing the stereotypes that people have heard growing up. It is a trip.

Ken: Here is another example of something to keep in mind in this discussion on differences. I was speaking once to a camp gathering of two thousand boys – half from the inner city and half from the suburbs. During one free time, some of the boys were being boys. Since there were no chandeliers in that rustic camp setting, they were working off some energy by jumping from one cabin roof to another. When one of them almost fell to the ground, I exclaimed, without thinking, "Jesus Christ! Are you trying to kill yourself?"

The white adults there looked at me in unbelief. Some of them wrote me later and asked, "Why did you swear?" Not immediately making the connection, I found myself wondering, *When did I swear?* I honestly did not remember swearing at the camp.

As I followed up, one of them clarified, "You used the Lord's name in vain."

That certainly did not sound like me. I asked him, "When did I do that?"

He responded, "You said, 'Jesus Christ' when the boy nearly fell from the roof."

In many sectors of the black community, that means *Jesus, help me.* I learned, however, that white Christians do not think in the same terms. I thought to myself, *Lord, 600 kids were saved that night. Another 300 rededicated their lives. It was a wonderful time, and what they remembered was I said 'Jesus Christ.'* That blew me away.

I shared with Ray, "I have learned that when I say that to a white audience I have to tell that story because people still get offended." In fact, I have found it helpful to change my vocabulary when I am in a different culture. You see, I am still learning.

Cultures Are not God-Ordained

We need to accept the fact that our cultures are different. In a so-called traditional black church, you have not preached unless you "whoop." On the other hand, if you whoop in some white churches, they will wonder, *What in the world?!? Has he lost his mind?!?*

So, when a white pastor invites an African American church to worship with your congregation, you may have to prepare your flock, "Now listen, this is a different cultural experience. Black preachers whoop! I cannot do it, but tonight you're going to experience the whoop."

And vicè-versa`. When you bring a white pastor into your African American church, say, "Now he doesn't have much whoop in him. But he's my brother." Many differences are significant. At the same time, many are superficial. We need to get past the superficial stuff.

Ray: We often ask our groups to work on a little 10-minute exercise around carefully designed questions, such as,

> ➤ Tell me a time when you were discrimi-nated against.

We all have been discriminated against. The Lord discriminated against me. He did not give me that much hair, and he did not make me 6'2". We all face some things that just aren't fair. My childhood was a very unhappy one. I could claim to be a victim. You have your own set of injustices. Again, that simply means we have certain things in common. So, we should get into small groups and start talking about those things. Pain is pain. The devil tries to tell you that one pain is worse than another – just like he tries to tell you that one sin is worse than another. No! God hates it all.

Steps Three and Four. As your relationship develops, your self-disclosure will make you feel very vulnerable. Getting past those barriers is key to your growth. Let us give you a couple of examples at the risk of offending some. We want to be real with you. If we offend you, please forgive us. We feel this is a proper setting to ask some very sensitive questions. However, if you would be offended by seeing the *n-word* in print, just skip ahead to the next heading.

There are some things that a person of another culture cannot understand. I am thankful to have a friend like Ken. I ask him to help me understand some sensitive matters like,

> ➢ What does it feels like to be called n-word?
>
> ➢ What does it feel like when he and I have been in a department store together and he gets followed by a security officer?

Ken: From the outset, we have to understand that Christian unity involves the spirit, and those that worship God must worship Him in spirit and in truth. The n-word is part of a deeply entrenched tradition which originated in days of slavery.

Let me share with you an excerpt from a speech attributed to a bogeyman referred to in some places as Slick Willy and in other places as Willie Lynch. According to a reliable English language source, the speech is inconsistent with the literary style extant in 1712. It may be that someone fabricated the "speech" to fan the flames of animosity against the "white devil." Anyway, here is what the infamous consultant from the West Indies is said to have advised Virginia slave owners:

I greet you here on the River in the year of our Lord, 1712. First I shall thank you gentlemen, the Colony of Virginia, for bringing me here.... to help you solve your problems with your slaves.

Your invitation reached me on my modest plantation in the West Indies, where I have experimented with some of the newest and still oldest methods of control of slaves. Ancient Rome would envy us and my program, if implemented.

As our boat sailed on the James River, named for our illustrious King James, whose version we still cherish, I saw enough to know that your problem is not unique. Where Rome used cords of wood as crosses for standing human bodies along the old highways in great numbers, you are still using the tree and the rope on occasion. I caught a whiff of a dead slave hanging from a tree a couple of miles back. You are not only losing valuable livestock by hanging, but you're having uprisings and your slaves are running away, and your crops are sometimes left in the field for too long for maximum profit. You suffer occasional fires, and your animals are killed.

.... In my bag here, I have a foolproof method of controlling your black slaves. I guarantee that, if you implement it ... correctly, it will control your slaves for at least three hundred years. My method is simple, and members of your family and overseers can use it.

I have outlined a number of differences among the slaves, and I take the differences and I make them bigger. I use fear, distrust, and envy for control purposes. These methods have worked on my modest plantation ..., and they will work throughout the South for you also....

On the top of the list is age. But it is only there because it starts with "a." Second, use color or shade. Other factors include intelligence, size, plantation, ... whether slaves live in the valley or on the hill, east, west, north, or south, have fine or coarse hair, are tall or short.

.... I assure you that distrust is stronger than trust. Envy is stronger than adulation.... Black slaves, after receiving this indoctrination, shall carry it on and it will become self-fulfilling and self-generating for hundreds of years, maybe thousands. Do not forget to pit the old black male against the young black male.... You must use the dark-skinned slave versus the light-skinned slave.... You must use female versus male.... You must also have the Caucasian servants and overseers distrust all blacks, but it is necessary that the black slaves trust and depend on us. They must love, respect, and trust only us.

Gentlemen, these kits are the keys to control over them. Have your wife and your children use them. Never miss an opportunity. My plan is guaranteed. And the good thing about this plan is, if it is used intently and properly for one year, the slaves will themselves remain potentially, perpetually distrustful.

Thank you, gentlemen.

The Jesus Factor

This excerpt intends to help us come to grips with the spirit of distrust within the black community and where it started. I understand why my forefathers told me, "Do not trust white folk." My forefathers were descended from slaves. Their forefathers had told them, right or wrong, that some whites are this way or that way. Where did that stuff come from? The spirit of Slick Willy started it way back when. But, he forgot one thing – the Jesus factor makes us brothers and sisters. It makes trust stronger than distrust. It made hope stronger than all of that other stuff that tries to bind us. The Jesus factor breaks that curse. It breaks that evil spirit that is very much alive.

Ray: As your relationship develops, so does your self-disclosure. You will become more vulnerable in that process. You will begin to talk beyond surface things, about the real issues of pain; and you will get beyond your comfort zones.

Let me just give you a couple of action points. First, minister to each other for the purpose of converting that pain from possible bitterness and anger into brokenness. That gets back to the very first thing that we shared. We have a common poverty, and that is our brokenness before Christ. Brokenness will lead to humility, which is vital to reconciliation. Reconciliation will develop your sensitivity to God and to others.

Ken: Here is a significant observation Ray made when we were in Atlanta together. I had never noticed this before. We were at Five Points, right down near the Dome. It is a 98 percent African American community. Because we have such an open relationship, Ray felt he could raise an issue with me, "Ken, every time an African American walks by, even though he is a stranger to both of us, he acknowledges you but not me."

I said, "Man, get out of here. You're 'tripping'." Ray told me to observe what was going on. I began to notice that African American brothers were doing just that.

In fact, now I notice it wherever we go together. African Americans, even though they are strangers to each other, will often acknowledge one another and exchange a greeting such as, "What's up?" – a colloquialism that means simply, "Hello." It does not seem to matter where they are. African Americans will tend to address the African American, often ignoring other parties who may be present.

I thought maybe it was because I was walking on the outside toward traffic. So, I moved to the inside. Still, people would look past him every time. I counted 19 instances in a row. So I devised an experiment, "Let's do this. Every time they look at me, I am going to look at you; and they'll have to acknowledge you."

That pattern Ray observed comes from the slavery experience. Slaves were not allowed to look whites in the eye; such behavior was considered a form of disrespect. Slaves began to look to each other to get respect. Therefore, that has been passed down through the years. Since it is subconscious, we can teach a different approach.

Many white people have been conditioned not to look at African Americans as they pass them on the street or in a hallway. So, I say *hello!* warmly when they do not look at me. Much of the time, they continue to look away even though they feel obliged to respond with their own *hello*. It blows them away when I do that.

When we would go into restaurants together, Ray would note, "Watch this. They're going to ask me for my order first every time." He was right. They also ask for his autograph to pay the bill every time. (I like that part.) Whenever we go into a restaurant – whether it is black, Hispanic, or white – whoever the waiter or waitress is – they do not even know they are doing it. Ray deals with it this way, "No, honor my brother first." It blows them away.

We have made a conscious decision that we are going to call attention to certain cultural practices that are demeaning. We are not going to allow that stuff to happen when we are together.

In church, once you introduce yourself to somebody you often grab hands and try to make eye contact. Some African Americans feel very uncomfortable with doing that. You, as a white person who knows that, can help them feel more comfortable. When they look down, just lift their hands up. Get their gaze. Let them know they are welcome in your church. That breaks down walls that have been built up culturally and historically. That's intentionality.

Ray and I ask questions like: Why did that happen? What can we do to break that pattern? How can we train our children? How can we train our next generation to be reconciled to do it the right way? How can we all come together and do this thing the right way?

Ken: I have to really check myself on certain things even today. In the community where I grew up, it seemed like n-word was my name. Almost everyone I would meet would greet me with, "What's up, N-word?" It was a term of endearment. However, I am going to tell you. If Ray were to call me n-word, we would have to fight. My wife says, "If it is wrong for Ray, it is wrong for you to say, too."

I know. Wrong is wrong. I am going to tell you, I had to be conditioned not to say *n-word* anymore. We do a lot of ministry in prisons. Many of the brothers in prison still use that term of endearment. So, I find myself fighting use of the same terminology in the midst of trying to discourage them from using the word.

As another example, when you go to a place like Texas, some white guys call brothers (adult male African Americans) *boy.* That is very inflammatory. You should not call a brother "boy." Even though it is a term of endearment when used in the proper context, the term carries so much baggage from the days of slavery and Jim Crow that it is a big insult to call an African American man a boy without his permission. That is the crux of the double standard in the use of this emotion-laden term. African Americans have implicit permission to refer to each other as *boy.* Whites have to earn the right to enter into that inner sanctum.

How, then, can you come to understand and appreciate that seemingly innocent words can be offensive? Simply talk about it with your African American friends. When you get a better understanding of such matters, you have a better chance of developing cross-cultural sensitivity.

Ray: Ken is bringing up a very good point. I know that a number of people are offended if I say the n-word. Many of my African American brothers do not say the word because of their comfort factor and how it affects them personally. The reason I say the entire word in training sessions is because I want to display to clients that there is enough trust in the relationship between Ken and me that it is okay. I understand that I could very well offend many, but we are trying to give you a working model of how, when your relationship moves beyond a point, you and I would have the permission to say that word because we know each other's heart. I have deep respect for my brothers and sisters and would not say the word in ordinary conversation. When I used it, it was in the sense of, "Help me understand how this word wounds my brother when it is spoken."

Ken: Ray has noticed that African Americans say it to one another all the time. I understand that white people say it to one another and seem to be comfortable with it. Now why is it so much more offensive when whites say it to African Americans? And why is my wife getting into the fray? But that's good. She is right, as usual. Wrong is wrong. It is degrading terminology, even though some may use it as a term of endearment. There are different *druthers* all over the place. It is a similar matter when some brothers call ladies the "b-word" with affection, "She's my 'b-word'." Some women feel esteemed by that.

My feeling is, "You call my daughter that, and I will slap you up side your head. You call my wife that; and we are gonna fight, Jack." So how does one get past the offense when someone of a different ethnicity uses a term which is considered endearing when used within your group? I would recommend dropping such terms from everyone's vocabulary. What purpose does it serve to turn some of your brothers against you?

Ken: The n-word derived from the fact that most Caucasian people could not pronounce Niger, a word which means black and is the name of one of the countries from which the slaves were taken.

Ray: The other possible term of origin is *nega*, which means "brother-man." The slave traders heard this word being used on the ships. When they tried to duplicate it, they got it all messed up.

Ken: It is somewhat similar to the drinking issue. You cannot find in the Bible that drinking is a sin. Getting drunk is sin. However, if drinking offends your brother, the Bible encourages you not to drink publicly, if at all.

Ray: Let me jump to step five. As Ken and I move through this relationship, it is obvious that there are differences between us. Being united does not mean being identical. Unity is not sameness. No matter what – I am not going to be black; and Ken is not going to be white. So why would I try to be black? Why would he try to be white? Let's just be who we are. In fact, let me make this point very clear. Ken is my best friend, but not *because* he is black. Ken is my best friend, and he *happens* to be black.

Our friendship has developed to the level that it has because we are committed to the relationship. It is not that he is my trophy or I am his trophy. Many people make a point of saying, "Some of my best friends are black." Or, "Some of my best friends are white." So what? Just because you are sitting in a garage does not make you a car. The point is that the friendship is based on the relationship. Ours just happens to be a cross-cultural one. Ken and I were not walking around with signs saying:

Need a black friend here.

or

Need a white friend here.

God just brought us together. After noting the opportunity God had presented to us, we worked on developing our relationship in an intentional way.

Along with our differences, we each possess many valuable attributes. We each bring the uniqueness of ourselves, our cultures, and our experiences. A lot of things about me have rubbed off on Ken, such as organizational skills and other things that are part of my make-up. The reverse is also true. Thanks to Ken, I have learned to become a lot more laid back and relaxed. There are times now when I just kind of let it flow a little. Ken has told me to "chill out" so much that I am beginning to learn to do it. Guess what? I think I like it.

Ken: I have to agree with that principle of two-way cross-fertilization. Two years ago, I did not think highly of anybody who would take a club, go out on a golf tee, hit a little ball, and try to find it just to hit it again. I thought, *What idiot would want to spend a lot of time doing that?*

Then one day Ray told me, "Ken, you need to take golf lessons. Not only is golf fun and relaxing, you can also have good Christian fellowship, transact business deals, and have a ministry to other golfers."

I started thinking, *I like Ray because he's talented. I like talking with him, and I like hanging out together.* So I said, "Okay, cool."

Ray presented golf as an opportunity to accomplish a number of goals that are important to me. That was like icing on the cake. I would get to have fun and fellowship and in the process be able to minister, too. Good. I took the lessons, and now I am convinced.

Not long after I started golfing, my wife observed, "This game has got you." It sure has. I have swallowed the bait ... hook, line, and sinker. And it's all because of my friend, Ray. He has influenced me in this and in other things as much as I have influenced him.

I love working out. I bench press more than 400 pounds, and Ray was kind of jealous! So, for three years now he has been working out with me. We spend a lot of time in the gym together. I have encouraged him in the areas of weight lifting and running. He has gotten physically fit because of our relationship.

There are many things that we have each brought to the table. For one thing, we went into business together, a consulting practice. Ray is also on the board for my ministry. In fact, he has totally reorganized the whole process and the structure of our ministry. Our relationship has been beneficial for both parties.

Ray: I want to share another thing, particularly for our white friends. I have discovered that in the

Hispanic and the African American communities, there is a strong desire for physical closeness, where people hug and have a lot of contact. That is very foreign to most of us in the white community. Our idea of a casual contact is a simple "How are you, Sir?" But, I learned a different sense of community from interacting with Hispanics and African Americans. And I like it.

In short, there are a lot of unique contributions that each person or each group brings to the table. These differences can become a great benefit for all concerned. More importantly, the interdependence we display will demonstrate the power of the Gospel to a watching world.

Ken: Here's a little writing I love. Ray gave it to me. Every time I go to a Caucasian church, I read it to the people. It speaks of black people first:

How come when I was born, I was black? As I grew up, I was black. When I get sick, I'm black. When I die, I'll be black.

But you (white people) – when you were born, you were pink. As you grew up, you were white. When you get sick, you are green. When you go out in the sun, you are red. When you go out in the cold, you are blue. When you die, you turn purple.

And you call *me* colored?

Ray: Let me share a quick story. Then I will share a word picture. After our relationship began developing, we discovered there are other people whose hearts are right and who want to know how to work intentionally at reconciliation. So we organized a little ministry called Reconcilers of Christ.

We had an opportunity last summer to speak to a group of 250 men in Evansville, Indiana. We were pleased to see God minister that weekend, and we had a great time. As we presented our material, however, we were not really sure if we were hitting home because even within the true Church, reconciliation is a very difficult subject.

The following week, while Ken and I were having lunch in downtown Indianapolis, a young man came up to us with a little tear running down his face. (We did not know him.) He greeted us and said,

> I just want you to know that I was down in Evansville last weekend and heard the two of you speak. I heard the illustrations you shared. I heard the examples and everything, and I watched your relationship. So many times speakers come in and talk about what we should do, but they are not really living it out themselves.
>
> As I sat over there in the corner of the restaurant, I watched how you did those things you taught. You had the waiter take Ken's order first. I watched how you two conversed. I watched all that stuff, and I just want to tell you that I am so blessed that you are living what you are saying and not just telling it.

God has really allowed our relationship to be a beautiful thing. As I said, we have both kind of grown on each other. One thing that happened to change me is that Ken and I had the opportunity to speak in Martinsville, Indiana, at their first ever Martin Luther King birthday celebration before all the racial tensions began to flare up in 1997. The churches and community leaders wanted to change their image.

A year and a half later, as I was doing an interview at the TBN television station in Indianapolis, the station manager mentioned to me,

Our family was at the rally last year in Martinsville. Out of everything that we have ever heard on reconciliation, we remember the M&M example more than anything. That little illustration meant so much to us.

I want you to experience the same opportunity that this lady's family benefited from. It is very effective in a group. To begin with, take one M&M in each of your two hands. Look to a person next to you and see if they have a different color M&M than what you have. Now what colors do you see around you? We see brown, yellow, blue, green, and red, and so forth. This is a test in patience and long-suffering. Bite one of those M&Ms so you can see half of the M&M. Now show it to the person on each side of you. What do you notice? They are all the same inside.

Ken: Resist jumping to the conclusion that God says we are all different on the outside, but we are all a bunch of nuts on the inside.

Ray: Seriously, the simple illustration is that once you get past the outer shell of who we think we are and see who God has created us as on the inside, we really are the same. Each of those M&Ms went through a different process. Some went through the red paint line. Some went through the blue paint line, and some went through the brown, yellow, or green paint line. They all began the same. They really all ended up the same, too.

Similarly, we may have different cultural experiences. We may have different spiritual heritages. We may have different family backgrounds, or economics, or whatever it is. However, we are all the same as creatures of God with lots of important things in common.

The Muslim Mystique

Ken: The real, absolute truth regarding why the Muslim influence is becoming so huge in prisons is that they have found a responsive chord, and they harp on it over and over. Their evangelization program is built around what the white man did to us during slavery, the Jim Crow era, and even now. Who can deny that these atrocities were perpetrated on us – that we are feeling the cumulative effects of four centuries of prejudice, discrimination, and worse? The brothers in the institutions respond to that approach.

In our community, the barbershop is a place where a tremendous amount of philosophizing goes on. You will find a number of philosophical preachers in the barbershops. I read a writer's account of spending most of his adult life trying to understand, from an African American perspective, the injustices that the white man had perpetrated on the black man. After a long search, he reported how God touched him with a revelation of what really had happened. While quite interesting, his conclusions are not necessarily shared by everyone.

This man decided to share that new-found insight with the crowd at the local barber shop, beginning with a provocative question, "Who is really to blame for what we have gone through?"

He noted that the men in the barbershop went on and on talking about the white master keeping us down. When he could not take it any more, he took over the floor, "Brothers, we blame the white man for everything." They knew that he was a preacher, so they listened to him respectfully. "But our real problem is with God, not with the white man." That got their attention. All eyes were on him as they waited to hear how he would explain this outrageous statement. "We are indeed descendants of ancient Egyptians," he continued. "We were in power in Egypt for 3000 years. We were scientists, inventors, educators, and writers."

They liked that. Whenever you talk about blacks being descendants of a great civilization in ancient Egypt, you get people's attention because we have been put down for so long that whenever we hear anything that gives us validation, we perk up.

Then the writer added, "But that also means that we were among the first slave masters. We enslaved Israel for 400 years." They were surprised. "We were on the top, but now we are not because we picked a fight with God." Now they were even more surprised. Noticing a Bible on the counter, the speaker picked it up. (Even with the Islamic influence in the black community, most blacks still respect the Bible.) He started reading some verses from Isaiah 19:4 that spoke about God's judgment on Egypt because of idolatry, witchcraft, and sorcery. He talked about the idols and the worship in Africa. Then he showed them the first mention of slavery:

> I [God] will hand the Egyptians over to the power of a cruel master, and a fierce king will rule over them.

They cried in disbelief, "You mean that God permitted that to happen?"

"Yes," the speaker responded. "He also permitted disaster to happen to Israel and any other nations who turned from Him."

But the real bomb dropped when he got to the ships in Ezekiel 30:9, "In that day, messengers shall go forth from me [God] in *ships* to frighten Cush [Ethiopia] out of her complacency. [emphasis added]"

"The Lord sent the ships to pick us up," the preacher said quietly, waiting for everything to sink in. "He raised up the white man to bring the ships to pick us up and enslave us." There was absolute silence in the barbershop.

One of the men, who was also a minister, asked to see the text with his own eyes. He confirmed to everyone, "It's in there." They were shocked!

The missing piece of the puzzle was still needed, however – the vexing of the heart of the white man. So, the speaker decided to continue in Ezekiel. "Now I want to tell you why the white man cannot stand us," he said as he read on:

> I will vex the heart of many people when I shall bring thy destruction among nations in the countries which thou has not known.

"God vexed the white man's heart against us. That means," he said soberly, "that God is irritated at us." That was the knockout punch. The barbershop got so quiet you could hear the parking meters ticking outdoors.

The truth is that the white man does not owe me an apology. *We* need to get right with God, because – if the truth were known – we were among the first oppressors. Our ancestors – our ethnic group – were among the first to enslave people. So if we want to start pointing the finger and talk about what *the whites* did and what *their people* did, let's go ALL the way back. We cannot just start with slavery in America. We have to start with the whole truth and nothing but the truth. It is a God thing. It has nothing to do with skin. We have turned our back on God.

Persecution is a judgment from God. So, if you want to be mad at somebody, be mad at God. If you want to have somebody to blame, stop pointing the finger at the white man. He is not the real source of the problem. We turned our back on God. That is the problem. We cannot make this a skin thing. It is a sin thing. Again, that is why I like my T-shirt which says, "It's not a black thing; it's not a white thing; it's a Jesus thing. Enough said."

That is the real issue. Therefore, we African American ministers and preachers have a responsibility to tell the rest of the story once we hear it. Now you, reader, also have that responsibility. That is why we emphasized intentionality.

Sometimes we can our positions to tell truth. Coming from my white brother, certain concepts would be hard for African Americans to hear. Likewise, a white brother can stand in front of some white audiences and say certain things because they will be better able to receive them from him.

That is why we decided that sometimes we have to go as a team. Ray can say some things to the whites and I can say difficult things to the blacks. Similarly, if you want to start reaching out into the community around your church, find someone who looks like and understands the people to whom you wish to minister. That is also what intentionality is. Some people ask, "How do we get black people to come to our church?" The first thing I ask them is if they have somebody that can relate to African American music. If so, I then ask them if the people in the congregation can deal with it.

Further, are you ready for other environmental adaptations that will need to be implemented? That to-and-fro rocking thing is real. Black folk are serious when they have church. They like to rock! What often happens is that some pastors will say, "Our folks do not like that kind of music" because they have got some "frozen chosen" people who insist, "We are going to sing just like the Apostles did. None of that new-fangled music for us." They are totally oblivious to the fact that much of the music of the faith had its origin in the singalongs of the pubs and other very secular activities so that the music was in the vernacular of the people.

The bottom line is that you have to be sensitive to the cultural needs of the people in your mission field and create an environment conducive to bringing them in to hear the message. Quite frankly, when you create the right environment, they will come.

If you have all whites on staff, get some brothers who *are* brothers, not some brothers who are black but whose preferences are consistent with the cultural trappings of the white community. Get some straight-out brothers who know how to deal with both cultures. Conversely, if you have an all-black staff, recruit a white fellow who understands the white community – not one who grew up in the 'hood. You must enlist someone who understands his ethnic group, who understands what they want, what they like to eat, and so forth. Use this person as a bridge in bringing the rest of the group into fellowship with you.

Ken: That is the way we started reaching out in my community. We found that many inter-racial couples were not comfortable going to an all-black church. Nor were they comfortable going to an all-white church. God brought our hearts together. We started saying that we simply open doors. It is up to the people to come in. We have a sign at the church that says,

Prostitutes, homosexuals, gang members – all welcome.

Sincerely,

Jesus

After we started meeting together, I came to an interesting revelation. It is not that blacks are striving for reconciliation; they are striving for recognition. There can never be reconciliation until there is recognition. It is not that blacks want white people to say they are sorry because of slavery, but to say they are sorry because of not recognizing us as human beings. You have to realize we are the same as you; and you are no better than we.

This means you are going to have to challenge the greatest myth that has put America on its back – that white people are superior to black people. It is in the church today – and, unfortunately, not just in the pews. Many white pastors do not think they can learn from black pastors. Before the groups can be reconciled, whites have to recognize that blacks have a contribution to make, also. Too often, our white brethren invite us to come over to their place and learn from them while there is no thought that they could learn anything from the black Christians. That attitude is a direct descendant from the mentality that brought racial injustice about in the first place.

I came to learn that, at first, it did not occur to Ray that I could bring anything to his congregation. However, after we talked some, he began to realize that an African American Christian could be an asset to a predominantly white congregation in a mixed community.

I was going to be who I am. I had no intention of changing, and it was clear that Ray saw no need to change. That was not the end of it, however. In the end, we both changed because we recognized he had something that I needed, and I had something that he needed. The white church will not become all that God intends until you get what the black community has to give you. We will not grow until we each learn that we each have something that the other needs.

I did not jump at the first invitation to join Ray's church. I was not going there as if it was the Promised Land. I fussed with God for a whole year about going. I wondered if the Lord knew that the church was all white and I was black, that I was an expressive Pentecostal and they were very reserved in their Christianity.

When I decided to attend Ray's church, it changed his church; but not right away. I would go in there and say *hallelujah* and tell the speaker to *preach!* At first, some in the congregation looked at me like, *Hum, do we have to act like that?* But today, his Church has made a revolution. They say *hallelujah* voluntarily now, even when I am not present. They are learning to clap their hands. What happened? They found out that it is just fine for me to express myself; and it is fine for them to express themselves if they so desire.

I am really saying that they recognized *me*. They acknowledged *my* dignity, *my* worth. As long as I have to keep trying to prove to someone that I am a person of worth, we can never get together. But once the other recognizes that I am a child of God, just like them – with unique contributions that the Church needs and vicè versà – then we are on the road to what the Bible calls reconciliation. Together we stand, and divided we fall. We leave you with this prayer.

Father God, we love You, and we thank You for truth. We have tried to cram so much into this chapter. There is so much we need to talk about and learn. But Father God, we thank You for these seeds, and we hope that others will be blessed through reading about the uniqueness of the relationship between Ray and myself and how we attempt to live out what Your Word says we must be.

Father God, we know that it is not brain surgery. It is not something that is so out of the ordinary that people cannot follow the example set by Jesus. Thank You for the practicality of Your admonition to study to show ourselves approved workmen who rightly divide the Word of Truth.

I pray for every situation that is represented among our readers – the pastors, the lay leaders, and the individuals who have a vision to bring our peoples and our churches together. We know that You have birthed this vision in them. Make the visions inside them become reality as a result of what we have written.

Father, may we understand that we are living out Your purpose, Your vision, Your command to go into the world and make disciples of all nations – all ethnic heritages and groups – baptizing them in the name of the Father and of the Son and of the Holy, mighty Spirit of God.

So, Father, we thank You for what you are going to do and what You have begun in our lives. May this book be a source to water the seeds that have been implanted in our psyche, our soul, and our mind. And, Father God, when that happens, may we be careful to point people back to the cross and give You all the glory, all the honor, and all the praise; for it is in Jesus' magnificent name we pray. Amen.

5 – The Church of Jesus Christ Is One

– Alex Montoya [1]

D r. Ware is to be commended for being one of the few brave souls in America attempting conferences and ministries to reunite the people of God with integrity. I personally want to thank Dr. Ware for his courage, for his vision, and for the opportunity to be a part of what he does. I am grateful that God raised him up and gave him this burden, this challenge, that America must face.

Trends in America

There are two trends I want you to consider as a preface to this chapter. The first is that by the year 2020, America is destined to be over 50 percent minority. More precisely, by the year 2020, America will no longer be considered a white Anglo-Saxon

---

[1] Dr. Montoya is senior pastor of First Fundamental Bible Church of Monterey Park, California, as well as founder and president of the Southern California School of Ministry, a bilingual institution working primarily among Hispanics. He is Associate Professor of Pastoral Ministries at Master's Seminary. The author of *Hispanic Ministry in North America*, he has planted 15 churches in California.

community. The United States will be composed of a number of ethnic groups, neither of which will constitute a majority by itself. That is not something to dread. It is just something to face. In a real sense, it is just another challenge in a world of ambiguity characterized by change.

The second trend that we need to reckon with is also social in nature. You may recall that in the 1960s, the theme of America was integration – let us come together. The theme of the 1990s was separation. We found this theme alive and well in the Church also. There were well-meaning and not-so-well-meaning voices encouraging us to develop homogeneous assemblies. They called church planters to identify our distinctive cultures, then separate, creating homogeneous churches along the same lines as the world's homogeneous communities.

These trends are presenting us with a two-horned dilemma: We have, on the one hand, the necessity of integration and at the same time the necessity of celebrating the fact that we do have distinct subcultures even within our own cultures. Because there are so many aspects to this issue, it is difficult to address the topic in a limited space. Nonetheless, I will focus my comments on trying to resolve this issue.

What if we do have homogeneous assemblies? What if that is going to be the issue, not only for the 90s, but also for the first half of the 21st century? What do we do about the matter? The problem that we have before us is two sided. The first part is this: If we do have racially distinct congregations, if we polarize ourselves – there will be a tendency for some

of us to think that others are *not equal* to us. We may adopt a paternalistic attitude to other assemblies. We may begin to look down at others and say *our* community. We will be tempted to believe that *our* church is a better church than the other church down the street. We have seen that throughout the ages.

The flip side of that coin is for some of us to feel as if we are *inferior* to other assemblies. We may see the other congregation as having more money, a longer legacy, a greater heritage, and/or the like. So, members of the poorer or younger homogeneous church might feel inferior. That is one way we in the Church continue to polarize ourselves. We see ourselves divided, with some thinking they are inferior and others agreeing with them in their sometimes self-imposed feeling of inferiority. We do not have the unity and oneness that ought to exist in the body of Jesus Christ.

My purpose here is to address the issue of equality – the Church of Jesus Christ is one. Even if we do put ourselves into homogeneous communities, we still must recognize that we are one in Christ – that we are all equal. Let me draw your attention to the Word of God because His Word has the answer to all of our problems – not just to some of them. Look at Acts 11:19-30.

> Now they who were scattered abroad upon the persecution that arose about Stephen, traveled as far as … Antioch, preaching the word to … the Jews. And some of them were men of Cyprus and Cyrene, who, when they were come to Antioch, spoke unto the Greeks, preaching the Lord Jesus. And the hand of the Lord was with them; and a great number believed, and turned unto

the Lord.

> Then tidings ... came to the ears of the church ... in Jerusalem; and they sent forth Barnabas [to] Antioch, Who, when he came, and had seen the grace of God, was glad, and exhorted them all, that ... they would cling unto the Lord.... and many people were added unto the Lord.

> Then departed Barnabas to Tarsus, to seek Saul. And ... brought him unto Antioch. And ... for a whole year they ... taught many people. And the disciples were called Christians first in Antioch.

When the church heard about the great famine,

> ... every man according to his ability, determined to send relief unto the brethren who dwelt in Judea; Which ... they sent it to the elders by the hands of Barnabas and Saul.

This is a powerful word. I pray that the Father will help us to be people of the Book. May His Word be the standard for every one of us as the Father teaches us.

Antioch, the Model Church

I am impressed with the church in Antioch. It has the solution for us. This was a marvelous church – the church of a number of firsts. It was the first Gentile church, the first church where the disciples were called Christians. It was the first church to contribute to the Jewish believers. It was the first church to request a general church council to resolve a problem in the early church. It also became the first official missionary sending assembly. It is no mean church. It is a model church. It speaks to us today that God who sets the pattern will lift this church up before us now as an example for all of us to follow.

The church at Antioch is the model for us, speaking to us whether we are Jew or Gentile – whatever our nationality, whatever our racial background, whatever our homogeneous tendencies. It will speak to us on the matter of equality. If you and I read the Scriptures carefully, we will see that plainly. Let me give you a plea for equality. If we learn anything from the church of Antioch as it relates to other churches, it is that we are all the same. We are one Church.

Five Justifications for Equality. I hear five justifications for equality emanating from Antioch. The first is this – that all of us have the same *existence*. We were brought into existence by the same God. It is not by accident that you find in verse 21 that it says, "the hand of the Lord was with them and a large number who believed turned to the Lord." Verse 23 says again that when Barnabas arrived he witnessed the grace of God. The Church is God's Church. It is not man's Church. The Spirit of God says to us that the church at Antioch was started – not by the Apostles, not by Peter or John, not by the Apostle Paul – it was started by believers who were scattered out of the persecution that arose after Stephen was stoned for his faith.

We Are All God's Church. They took off in their "cars" and ended up in Antioch and started sharing the gospel at local Burger Kings and Taco Bells, so to speak. They apparently were so excited about the Good News that they could not keep it secret; and people came to faith in Christ. This church was nothing less than a miracle, a reminder that God is the author of the Church. Again, it is God's Church. We are reminded of what the Apostle Paul says in 1 Corinthians 3:5-7, where he tries to resolve the divisions in Corinth:

> What ... is Apollos? And what is Paul? Only ser-
> vants through whom you came to believe – as the Lord
> has assigned to each his task. I planted the seed; Apol-
> los watered it; but God made it to grow. So neither he
> who plants nor he who waters is anything, but only God,
> who makes things grow. We are God's fellow workers.
> You are God's field. You are God's building.

Then I would ask you, is God's Church divided? A thousand times no! Paul speaks of the Church as the Body of Christ. The eye cannot declare independence from the feet, nor the hand from the rest of the body. We are not divided.

Sometimes we who are ministers speak of "our" church. We talk about "Dr. McArthur's church." We speak of "Dr. Hill's church" or "Dr. Romero's church." No, my friends. It is God's Church. We ought never forget that. So, when you drive down the street and see a church that has Korean writing or Spanish words, remind yourself that it is God's Church. God is the author and the builder. It belongs to the Lord Jesus Christ. That should speak volumes to us. Neither you nor I should ever usurp the authority God has placed in His Church. Antioch was not a Gentile church, but God's Church.

Are We Christians? Let me give you a second justification for equality. After Barnabas and Paul had spent an entire year teaching there, Acts 11:26 says

that the believers were first called Christians in Antioch. Before that, they were just unnamed disciples,
followers of the way, followers of Jesus. Now the
Spirit of God tells us that they were first called
Christians in Antioch. Imagine that!

The word "Christian" is only found three times in
the Scriptures. Later on, you will recall that Agrippa
said to Paul, "Almost thou persuadest me to become
a Christian" (Acts 26:28). In another place, Peter says
to the saints scattered throughout Asia Minor, "if you
suffer as a Christian, do not be ashamed, but praise
God that you bear that name" (1 Peter 4:16).
Americans have gotten so used to the term that even
unbelievers call themselves Christians. At first, it was
used to refer to the Gentile believers of Antioch – not
the Jewish Christians in Jerusalem. Note who called
them by the lofty name of Christians. These Gentile
believers were so like Christ – they so loved the Lord
Jesus – they so behaved like Christ – that the
unbelievers called them Christians.

Sometimes you and I who live in North America
think that because we use a Ryrie Study Bible,
because we own a Scofield Bible, or sing a couple of
Dr. Watts' hymns – that we have a corner on
Christianity. May I remind you that there are
Christians all over the world who love Christ, who
belong to Christ, who are bought by Christ! They are
Christians, also. If you and I keep that in mind, we will
project a common identity to the world.

But, here is our problem, friends. I fear that Christ
is not the most important thing for us. Some of us are
Americans before we are Christians. We will salute
the flag before we honor the cross. We will sing the

Star Spangled Banner before we sing *The Old
Rugged Cross*. Do not get me wrong; I love America.
I am an American. Before I am an American,
however, I am a Christian. This world is not my home.
I am just passing through. I have a six- by three-foot
piece of property in California; but I have a mansion in
heaven.

We talk about the black church, the white church,
and the Hispanic church; but we are using incorrect
terminology. We ought to be talking about Christ's
Church. We have a common denominator – that we
are identified by a common name. We are Christians.
That is the great equalizer for all of us.

Are you a Christian? That is all I need to know. I
do not need to know how much stock you own. I do
not need to know which side of the tracks you live on.
I just need to know that you belong to Christ. If so,
then as we say where I come from, *Bongala* (Let's
shake hands). You and I are brothers in the Lord
because we have a common identification. Maybe as
you read this, you are an American first and a
Christian second. You might be ethnic first and
Christian second. If that is so, you have a bad case of
near-sightedness. You can only see as far as the end
of your nose. You cannot see my nose.

We Are Interdependent. Let me give you the
third justification for equality. In Acts 11, you will find
that something rather exciting takes place at Antioch,
leading to two problems: The first problem was that
so many people came to Christ at Antioch that the
church was filled with new believers. When Barnabas
showed up, he was so overwhelmed that he said, *My*

goodness, Lord. Look at all these people here. They are brand new believers. They are in the Church, and they do not even know John 3:16. We need to help them get started.

As Barnabas prayed about pastoring the emerging church at Antioch, he thought, *Wait a minute, I have to find help.* So, he went over to Tarsus and picked up his friend Paul whom he knew to be rather astute in the Scriptures. And, for a whole year, they spent time helping the church grow in the knowledge of Jesus Christ.

The Jerusalem church interacted with the church at Antioch. They were not in competition. They cooperated with one another. We call it interdependence. The Jerusalem church wanted to help the Antioch church; and they did.

Then something else happened. A prophet by the name of Agabus came to Antioch and said, *You know what? There is a great famine in the Roman Empire. A large number of brothers and sisters in Jerusalem are starting to lose their livelihood.*

Somebody has said that a recession is when your neighbor loses his job. A depression is when you lose your job. Antioch had a recession but Jerusalem had a depression. And now we see something miraculous, friend, something wonderful. The church at Antioch made a motion to help the church in Jerusalem. They collected a lot of money to help the brothers and sisters there. Why? Because they were **interdependent**. That is a true expression of *koinonia* (Christian fellowship centered around the risen Savior). I am in favor of having small and large gatherings where we are mixed together. However, it goes beyond that. It goes down to real *koinonia*, where we do more than just sing and sit together. It is when we get down and work together.

In 1972, I was a pastor in East Los Angeles in the middle of a Hispanic community. We had forty members, all brand new believers. These new Christians could not find the book of Malachi. In fact, they could not even pronounce Malachi. Some called it Ma-laa-chee. Some called it *mariachi*. They could not even identify who Malachi was. I said, "Oh Lord I need some help here." I gave the old Macedonian call to brothers and sisters with the Navigators up in Washington, Montana, and Idaho, "Come on down and give us a hand."

Forty white brothers and sisters came down to East LA and spent four to six weeks with us for each of three summers. They did exactly what Barnabas and Paul had done for the church at Antioch. They helped us to advance the cause of Christ. That is another version of what I mean by *koinonia* – participation in something we have in common – in this case, spiritual growth in Christ. That is true *koinonia*.

We all ought to give back and do whatever we can to advance the cause of Christ. I have participated in five conferences in four months outside my ministry at the Master's Seminary and my full ministry at our church. All the conferences have been outside the Hispanic community. They have been with our Anglo brothers in Seattle, Idaho, and northern California. Why is that? Because we share something in common. It is my turn to help other people, my turn to reciprocate because we all need one another. No man can do it alone. Similarly, no church can do it alone.

If you think you can do it alone, you are sadly mistaken. Oh, we have some pastors out there who are *solo lobos* (lone wolves). *This is my church. I will do it my way.* I have news for you, friend. In the wild, the lone wolf dies. Maybe that is why your church is dying, dear pastor, because you are a lone wolf. You need people. You need me, and I need you. We were never made to be independent. We were made to be interdependent.

You see it in the church at Antioch. They did not respond to Agabus that the Jerusalem church's problems were their own – that they had their own challenges in Antioch. They had a more spiritual attitude, *Let's help them financially. We are indebted to them. They need us now.* That is what it is all about – interdependence.

I hope you do not have the attitude of a parasite. Parasites are takers. I hope you are not a giant leach who just robs a host of its life-giving substance and then leaves. I hope you have the attitude of asking if someone needs you and your expertise. I go to some churches where they have two or three wonderful pianos on stage with virtuoso pianists lined up to take their turns to play. I go to other churches and they cannot find a pianist to save their skin. Listen Mr. Pianist, Ms. Pianist. Find yourself a church and be the number one pianist, not the tenth pianist in line. They need you out there. Be interdependent.

I was talking to an Anglo pastor who was planting a church out in California. I told him that whenever he needed some musicians that he could take them from our church. *Take them with you. Let them sing at your place. That is what we are here for. At our church, they can only sing once a month or even once every two months. Get them out of here. Let them sing in your church. We do not own them. They are God's servants.* We need to do that, friends. Until your church is involved in the lives of other churches, you are not experiencing *koinonia*. We all have a common necessity; I need you, and you need me.

We Are All Saved By Grace

Let me hasten to the fourth justification for equality – the fact that we are all the same. I want to remind you of Acts 15, a record of the first Christian council. They met to resolve the following problem. There were numerous Gentile churches emerging all over the Empire. Paul and Barnabas had been sent out by the Antioch church and had started congregations all over the place. These were for the most part Gentile churches.

Some of the Jewish Christians began to wonder, *What do we do with them? They are not like us. They are not doing things the right way.*

Some of the people from the Jerusalem church said, *We need to call these churches in and tell them to get in line. We do not like the way they sway with the music. We do not like the way they use guitars in their worship.*

A council was convened to decide what to do with this so-called Gentile church. When it was all said and done, the council concluded: *They are saved by the same blood that saved us. They have the same spirit that we have. They are the same.*

I call it equality of recognition. The Spirit of God put His stamp of approval on the church at Antioch and on all the other Gentile churches. They are real authentic churches. Our problem is that we want everyone to do it our way. However, God affirms their way, too. God said that these Gentile churches do not need the Mosaic Law. They do not need to be circumcised. They are not Jews. Leave them alone. If the Jewish church wants to be circumcised, let them be circumcised. If they do not want to be circumcised, they do not have to be circumcised. Both decisions are OK. God affirmed them both. However, we choose to let issues like that divide us. When it comes to culture and preferences in the nonessentials, we should let each church choose its own way.

Some churches are so methodical. They begin the service at 9 o'clock sharp. At 10:08, they have the closing stanza. And it ends with the threefold amen at 10:10 sharp. I came from an educational institution like that. They taught us like that. So, one day I decided to do that in a Hispanic church. We were going to begin the service right at 9 o'clock. I had the pianist lined up. I had the choir lined up – all three of them. We began the service when the clock began to chime. Guess what? We had nobody there! In the Hispanic culture, people just do not come at 9 o'clock. They come when they want to come (if you understand where I am coming from). I had the first hymn at 9 o'clock, the second hymn and the announcements at 9:05. At 9:10, we took the offering. However, there was nobody there. Then after we collected only about $45 for the offering for the second week, I concluded quickly, *We are going to go broke at this rate.* That lasted only about two weeks. Now we conduct worship services according to our Hispanic culture, which views life as an event, not a schedule. This also means that I do not have to end my sermon at 10:10. I can end it at 12:10 if I want to.

In fact, when I presented this address at the Third Multiracial Ministry Conference, Dr. Ware told me to close at 8:20 p.m. I told him I will close when *I* want to close. According to Hilbert and Johnson's chapter, Dr. Ware has got to recognize *my* identity, *my* culture. (I was kidding, of course.)

Sometimes we may believe that we cannot visit another church because we may not feel comfortable at that church. No, friend; it is just that you do not affirm them. That is all. You cannot listen to a nice European choir because you cannot affirm them. We have to learn to affirm them. You know – I am a Dr. Pepper man. When I go to a vending machine, I look for Dr. Pepper. I like Dr. Pepper. That does not mean that Coke is bad or Sprite is bad. I do not spit into a Pepsi can. I just prefer Dr. Pepper. Do you like Coke? Great! You want Sprite? Good for you. We need to have an attitude of affirmation with one another. An equality of recognition. The Spirit of God accepts our diversity. So should we. That is what the Jerusalem council was all about. Leave them alone, Jacob. God affirms them.

We Are Co-laborers. Let me lay before you a fifth justification. There is a powerful section in Acts 13,

> In the church in Antioch there were prophets and teachers: Barnabas, Simeon who was called Niger, Lucius of Cyrene, Manaen who had been brought up with Herod the tetrarch, and Saul. While they were worshiping the Lord and fasting, the Holy Spirit said, 'Set apart for me Barnabas and Saul for the work to which I have called them.' So, after they had fasted and prayed, they placed their hands on them and sent them off. (Acts 13:1-4)

I call this equality of responsibility. Immediately following Pentecost, everything seemed to be about the Jerusalem church. Now the church at Antioch has been established and affirmed and has equal status. Now God says, *Since you have an equal status in the church at Antioch, I will give you equal responsibility. Now I am giving you lead responsibility in world evangelization. Now the Great Commission is yours, also. Oh, yes, I told the twelve to tarry in Jerusalem until they were clothed with power from on high to be my witnesses to the ends of the earth. But, Antioch, now it is your turn. From here on it is not Jerusalem, but Antioch, who has lead responsibility for world evangelization.*

Some of us would like to have equal privileges. Just do not ask us to be equally responsible. What God is saying to us here is, *I consider you all equal and you also have equal responsibility*. This church did not protest to the Spirit of God, *You know we cannot do this, God*. They did not use all the excuses churches often make. They did not say, *but God we*

*are a Gentile church. You cannot expect us to do
what the Jerusalem church is doing, can you?*

They did not say, *We are just too young. We have
only been around a short while.* They did not say that
they did not have the resources, the training, or the
money. They did not claim to be dysfunctional.

Let me tell you something, all you who feel you
are dysfunctional people. I have been around a while.
What I have learned is that we are all dysfunctional.
There is a saying in Spanish, "Among the blind, the
one-eyed man is king." God says, *You know, with all
the blind out there, you are going to be king.* There
are no excuses.

Now let me say a word to our Hispanic people
because so many of us make excuses. We must take
the responsibility of world evangelization, of sending
missionaries out, of supporting missionaries, of
raising up great ministries. Some folks call us a
Hispanic church; we are not a Hispanic church. We
are a Christian church. It just so happens that most of
us in our group are Hispanics. We have an obligation,
not to Hispanics alone; but to the world. We are
indebted, as was Paul, to the Jew and to the Gentile.
We are not excused.

Some of us suffer from an inferiority complex. We
think that that excuses us from the Great Commission. We are not excused. We just need to grow up.

Twenty-eight years ago, I came to First
Fundamental Bible Church when it was a small
church. When we outgrew our building, we had to find
a larger place. So, we needed to raise money.

However, I was afflicted with a complex of syndromes – the smallness syndrome, the immigrant syndrome. Therefore, I wrote a letter to 500 churches all across America because I had been taught that we belong to a great organization – the Church. I asked for their help. I asked them to send us some money to help buy a bigger facility because we were a poor church, a small church. If fact, I told them just that – that we were a poor, small church; and we needed their money. I signed all the letters carefully. I licked them all. I mailed them off. And I waited with great anticipation for these wonderful brothers to shower their money in our direction.

I was totally unprepared for the disappointment that followed. I got two responses back out of five hundred letters. *Two*! One of them said, "Dear Brother, Sorry I cannot help you." Another letter which came from another Pastor said, "Dear Alex, I know you need some help; and this is all I can give you: one dollar." I sat there with one dollar and thought

One dollar!!?!! Dear God, ONE DOLLAR!!?!! Five hundred letters produced one dollar!!?!! Who are these tightwads? Where is this koinonia stuff?

But God said,

Alex, grow up. Grow up. You have to carry the responsibility now. This being on the dole – forget it. Get your act together. Do what needs to be done. Your people and you need to rise to the occasion.

I learned a lot. I learned that the Church does not understand its interdependence yet. I also learned that it is Antioch all over again. Where there is a will, there is a way. Since then, we have started fourteen new churches and funded them ourselves. Brothers and sisters, we have a responsibility to the world because we are equal. We are not here to promote our own little con or our own agenda. We are not here to promote our ethnicity. We are not here to promote brownness or blackness or whiteness or yellowness. We are here to promote the Church of Christ. Under the cross of Christ, all of us stand absolutely equal. May it be so in your life and ministry.

6 – Suburban / Urban Church Partnerships

– James Lowther[□]

I got into Biblical reconciliation through Dr. Ware when he pastored a church near me. He sent his children to our school. One day he invited me to join a new organization called The Voice of Biblical Reconciliation. After a few meetings, I began to feel that I did not know nearly as much about this as I had thought. Under conviction, I began making some changes. This chapter addresses the fact that whatever we do needs to be purposeful, intentional, and accommodating.

One cannot just sit out in the suburbs with the attitude, "I am not prejudiced. They can come to our church if they want to." If you put forth no welcome, no invitation, and no effort, you are kidding yourself. That is a state of denial. The seminar I presented in

---

[□]Rev. James Lowther is senior pastor of Camp Springs Community Church in Clinton, Maryland, and president of the Voice of Biblical Reconciliation. He is vice president of the Independent Fundamental Churches of America, Delmarva Region, and member of its National Ethnic Relations Committee. He is also director of special events for the Freedom of Religion Coalition.

1996 was entitled "Where to Begin." This chapter follows up on that topic.

You may find it interesting to note that even those of us who are working on suburban/urban partnerships have had some bad experiences in this quest. Some say it is impossible to bring about effective partnerships. I like to hear that admission. Our God is the God of the impossible. It just tells me that I cannot do it in my flesh, but we know that whatever is the will of God can be done in the power of Him who strengthens us.

So, let me begin with a little bit of the history and background. The Voice of Biblical Reconciliation is headquartered outside of Washington, D.C. Washington is an intriguing area in which to minister. It is really the front line. If Satan's seat is not there, it is pretty close. There are many things that we are battling out there, but the Lord is going to have His way.

Our church, Grace Community Church, is a member of the Independent Fundamental Churches of America (IFCA). If you are not familiar with IFCA, I might mention that Dr. John MacArthur, the prominent radio preacher and seminary president, is an IFCA pastor, also.

Our work with suburban / urban church partnerships is not limited to IFCA churches, however. For example, Fourth Presbyterian Church took the lead in suburban/urban church partnerships in our area. Fourth Presbyterian is the church that many of the politicians attend. By way of information, Cal Thomas, the commentator, attends that church. It is the church which Dwight Eisenhower attended when he was in Washington. When Dan Quail was vice-president, he attended that church. A congregation of 2500, it is located in Bethesda, MD, a very rich section of metropolitan Washington.

They used to be downtown. After they relocated to Bethesda, they still wanted to have an impact downtown. Therefore, they went back and formed a partnership with Star of Bethlehem. They did it the hard way, however, instead of doing some research first. They had never heard of Raleigh Washington and Glen Kehrein or any of the other people working in this area. They just jumped into it and found out it was not as easy as they thought it would be. They probably assumed that Christian people could get together, that there should be no problems.

The reality is that there are different cultures in different parts of America. (Anthropologists might prefer to call them different subcultures since we are all part of the American cultural mosaic.) There are different backgrounds and different ways of thinking. For example, people in the urban African American church often think about time differently than people in Bethesda. They tend to think differently about other matters as well, including resources, priorities, and organization.

Now let me pose an important question. If one is going to be a doctor or lawyer, it takes years of study and practice. If one is going to get into a marriage, it also takes years of understanding and hard work. Why do we think we are going to go downtown into an inner city context and sit down and say something meaningful without any preparation − without any resources? Why do we think we are going to somehow make a difference? It is not going to happen. The same type of effort that you put into a marriage or a profession has to be put into reconciliation – perhaps even more so because you have the added opposition of spiritual warfare. Further, try as we might, we cannot put this preparation on our timetable. God has His own timetable. People seem to have their own timetable, too.

There are two pitfalls to avoid in the area of time. The first is **procrastination**. You have to move forward in spite of the fact that we understand that the task is a difficult undertaking. The second pitfall involves **scheduling** when we will be done with reconciliation. In many endeavors, we can set up a calendar of milestones and target dates. When it comes to reconciliation, we are going to have to develop the relationship before we can develop the partnership. Relationships cannot be scheduled. This is a concept which must be understood.

Not recognizing some of the dynamics involved, Fourth Presbyterian went downtown and brought in a tutoring program, a soup kitchen, clothing distribution, and a jobs partnership program. Our congregation began to get involved as well. There was a low-income housing program where a church could buy a run-down house for one dollar, or rent it for one dollar a year. Then they would renovate it and get a low-income family to move in. HUD has stopped this program, and that is unfortunate.

The Word was an important part of that partnership. Fourth Presbyterian arranged for pulpit exchanges.

Our church is also part of the Camp Bennett program where we take inner-city youths out to a camp in the country. We provide the counselors. My people came back from one camping experience saying, "Boy, I did not know how much ministry can happen in one week!"

We collaborated with an African American church during the camp. The African American church took the lead in counseling the young campers, and it was amazing. There are still children from that camp calling our counselors, looking up to them, and attending our church now and then. A couple of them are in our AWANA program. It is a wonderful thing. As Dr. Bartlette points out in his chapter, these urban youth had never seen white people reach out and try to help them before.

Now we are going to move from interpersonal relationships on out. These comments are addressed to my Anglo brothers primarily, but the same concepts apply where the African American church is concerned. You cannot reach across the line until you develop personal sensitivity. Many times we think, "I am not prejudiced. With my academic training and Fortune 500 experience, I am going to go in there and we are going to establish a state-of-the-art program." The way we Anglos typically work (I know I am stereotyping; I am sorry) is we go to an exploratory meeting with a fully thought-out plan in our hip pocket. We have maps, charts, paradigms, and elaborate measures of success. We take all this structure and overlay it over the city and expect everything to fall into place.

Did you know that individuals do not fall into paradigms easily? They do not fall into charts. They do not fit into statistics. And we wonder why superior organizational design is not creating successful relationships. I hate to be the one to tell you. Organization is not relationship. You can have all the organization you want. It does not work by itself. The relationship has to come before the organization.

Now let me tell you some of the things I have been doing. One will not do well in cross-cultural relations with preconceived ideas. I have decided that part of this is not only personal contact and working, but also doing some research. Therefore, I started consuming biographies of African Americans, Native Americans, and other groups. I wanted to learn about their walk. I went through Mandela's story[2] in South Africa, as well, in order to gain a broader exposure to the world in which some of my brothers live. I started devouring those biographies and finding out about the people. The more I learned, the more questions I developed. I began going to my African American brothers, asking them to give me some honest answers.

We cannot be shocked by what we hear when we develop cross-cultural relationships. Here is a typical

---

[2] Nelson Mandela, *Long Walk to Freedom.* The autobiography of Nelson Mandela. Little, Brown. 1994.

Anglo approach. When we begin to get serious, we say, "We see the problem. So, let's forget about the past, brother, and move on from here."

The urban dweller generally objects to that proposed solution with a comment like, "But wait a minute, there is a lot of hurt back there."

The Anglo reasons, "But I was not the person who did it. Let's get on with our relationship."

No, no, no! If my attitude is the same as my ancestors, it is just as if I had owned slaves myself. There has to be an attitude of listening. We need some way that the urban brother can tell the suburban brother what is in his heart and mind.

As I read biographies and listened to books on tape about Thurgood Marshall, Martin L. King, Jr., George Washington Carver, and other, I always skipped Malcolm X because he had been a rabble-rouser. I thought that that guy was just a bad dude. That was the easy way to address unsettling information. In time, I realized that I had to learn about the whole spectrum.

What I learned affected the way I view Malcolm X. If my father and three uncles had been killed by white supremacists and my mother had been driven into a mental institution by harassment from white supremacists, I wonder how I would feel. The *Biography of Malcolm X* gave me a completely different perspective. I wondered how I would feel if the only place I could go to make money would be the underworld in Harlem. That biography got my thinking going about the shoes that these people walked in. Coming from a conservative, Anglo, Republican, pro-life community, I wonder what my politics would be like if I had to live in situations like those.

Therefore, I would encourage you to consume all kinds of literature and biographies that help you to understand the culture and ethnicity of the people you are going to work with. Do your homework.

An individual in my seminar pointed out how interesting it was to hear my comments about how to approach cross-cultural partnerships. Whenever their church sends someone out – say, to Muslim countries, but the same is true anywhere they go – one of the first things they do is try to learn about that culture, the way the people view their world, what their felt needs are, and as much as they can before they even go. When they minister cross-culturally, they find that Muslims are still extremely sensitive about the crusades. It is eye opening how tremendous an impact that atrocity still has on how Muslims view the West hundreds of years after the fact. The parallels to urban/suburban partnerships are most striking.

On a couple of occasions when I have gone down to Atlanta and some people have found out that I was from the North, they made it clear that they are still fighting the Civil War. That is the same type of perspective the Muslims are displaying.

I may not agree with everything that Bill Hybels does in the seeker-sensitive approach to Sunday worship. One thing he has taught us, however, is the fact that the culture is changing. We had better find out where the culture is if we are going to reach people. If they step into your church and feel like they have just stepped into the 19th century, do you think they are going to come back? Again, just as we are willing to invest thousands of dollars in cross-cultural sensitivity training before sending a missionary overseas, we had better find out what the culture is right up the street from us because it is different.

At the risk of stating the obvious, I hasten to add that overseas missionaries assume the role of learner and seek out a trust-worthy member of the target culture to provide continuing training in the unwritten dynamics of the culture. This should be instructive to us.

Our church is a scant 14 miles from the Capitol Building. People recognize that crossing that line – with the Anacostia River on one side and the Potomac coming from the other side – means crossing into a different world. If I am going to reach that world, I cannot step into it and just say, "Here I am." Bob Matthews, a true urban missionary, stood up at our coalition once and said,

> Many people will come in here with this great idea of what to do for Washington. They will do a blitz and get a lot of exposure and a lot of money. Then they will leave the city. Do you know what helps Washington? People who come and stay. *People who will live with the people.* [emphasis added]

Bob Matthews knows whereof he speaks. He has lived down there for 41 years – an Anglo guy in the middle of Southeast Washington, the roughest section of town. They trust him because he is not going in to do his thing and get out of town. So, if you want to do something, be there to stay. Do not do a shot and get out of town. It takes a commitment. We will talk about that more below.

First of all, here is a little bit of an *apologetic* theology. (Apologetics means a defense. It does not mean I am apologizing for something.) Why do we minister in the city? First of all, we are commanded to start with our Jerusalem, then our Judea, then our Samaria, and then the uttermost parts of the world (Acts 1:8). Your city is your Jerusalem. There has to be an impact there. This often requires significant investments of time, talent, and treasure. We need to send our most gifted communicators and support them with the prayer, finances, and other resources they need. After all, who – in his or her right mind – would enter a war and not do everything they could to win?

Number two, there needs to be meaningful interaction among all the members of the Body of Christ. When you go through 1 Corinthians 12, you see a number of different gifts. One of the sad things about segregation in the Church is we miss the opportunity to benefit from some of the gifts. We are missing an arm here, and we are missing a leg there. The Church was not designed to fragment; it was designed to come together. By the way, the *Reconciliation Recorder*, which we publish, has some articles on these issues. I also wrote a book called *Thunder in Antioch* which addresses the same things.

Thirdly, hospitality begins at home in the Body of Christ. "How can we say that we love Christ if we do not love our brother?" (1 John 4:20). John 13:35 says, "They will know you are my disciples if you have love for one another." *Love* is an active word. It involves reaching out, and not just to people who come across our path.

True discipleship is love in action. James 1:27 notes that true religion is helping marginalized people. Sam Heinz, of Third Street Church, who is with the Lord now, said, "You cannot truly say you love Jesus unless you help hurting people." There is some truth to that. Then, of course, the Bible also commands us to reach out to one another. If your brother comes and he has need, and you say, *Go and be warm and be filled brother, and you do not give him to eat, your faith is dead. Faith without works is dead* (James 2:15-16, 26).

Cross-cultural reconciliation requires an education process. This is something that I started understanding when I was dealing with Brother Ware and The Voice of Biblical Reconciliation. It is a fact that there is a lot of suspicion out there. There is a lot of hurt. You cannot just go in and say, "Hey brother, I am going to help you out."

They are probably thinking, "Yeah, sure you are." So, be careful. There has to be time to break down these barriers. There has to be something that shows genuineness. If you go in there and after a few months decide it is not worth it, they will say, "We told you so. You are not genuine." Do you know what you are trying to do? You feel guilty, so you are going to take your Bible and put an 'I have done a good work today' notch in it. If that is your attitude, you are not going to make it. It is not going to work.

Secondly, relationships will be tested.

Thirdly, those things that have been built up over the years are going to take a long time to straighten out. There are going to be problems. You have to build small areas of trust before expecting progress in greater areas. It is an incorrect approach to think, "We are going in and doing a massive partnership. We are going to meet together and give it three months to get this thing going." No, that is not going to work. You are not going to take a barrier that has been there for decades, tear it down, and in three months have a full-fledged partnership. If you try, someone is going to get hurt and hurt very badly. You know what happens quite often? Once they get burned, it is much more difficult the next time to start over again.

Misconceptions

There are a number of misconceptions that have to be broken down if we are going to move along.

Misconception Number One. Assume that all inner-city churches are liberal and emotion-based. Assume they are a bunch of liberals who do not preach the Gospel, that all they are interested in is having a good time, and then they will do food drives and stuff like that. Assume theirs is a social gospel. This perception is widespread in the IFCA.

Misconception Number Two. Similarly, many inner-city churches assume that white pastors are prejudiced and lack compassion for needy people. I am not saying that there is not a lot of this going on. I remember talking to a pastor downtown who said, "Listen, I went to seminary and the white guys did not want to have anything to do with me. So I said, 'Well I do not need *you* now, and I do not need you ever.

You stay on your side of the River; I will stay on my side.'"

There is a lot of that. You may wake up one day and say, "Ah, I have changed my mind. We need each other brother." Yeah. Right! Forget that. **Misconception Number Three**. Prejudiced people look for opportunities to confirm their prejudice. There are plenty of examples of liberal black churches. Likewise, there are countless examples of very uncompassionate white churches. However, we are not looking for examples; we are looking for Godliness. We are looking to break down strongholds of bad examples. James 4:17 tells us, "He who knows to do good and doeth it not, to him it is sin."

Misconception Number Four. Honest, open dialogue breaks down these barriers. That is partly true, but it takes more than that, as I have outlined above.

Inevitable Tensions

There are several tensions when you start to form a partnership. First, you are likely to be confronted by the evangelism versus social action tension. There is a tendency as we start a partnership with urban churches to allow the agenda to focus more on the area of helping the poor than reaching out. Do you know why? Because that is the most obvious *presenting* need. If I am in a middle-class suburban setting, I do not see a lot of people walking the street. I do not see many hurting people. However, they see them downtown. So, if the immediate need is to feed, clothe, and shelter hurting people, that is an easy choice for an emphasis.

When we began forming these partnerships, I sat down with the head of the partnership program and said, "Listen, if I am going to bring my white brothers down here from other churches, they are going to want to hear that we are also doing evangelism and discipleship." So many times white suburban pastors view urban churches as promoting a social gospel, while the true Gospel of Christ is not being presented. At the same time, many urban pastors question whether their suburban counterparts have any interest in social action. When we talk about putting partnerships together, therefore, we have to talk about this tension.

Often inner city pastors view white suburban pastors as being so heavenly-minded they are no earthly good. You will preach the Gospel but let someone starve at your doorstep. You will give them a tract as they breathe their last. The truth is, there is a need for both the Gospel of Christ and help for needy people. They are not mutually exclusive. After all, Jesus preached and then fed the 5,000. They go together. Any philosophy that is going to work needs to be centered around both of these concepts. Remember what Don Bartlette says in his chapter. The kind people fed him first. Then they taught him. *Then* he was able to hear the Word. Now, there's a novel concept!

The suburban church must also keep in mind that the urban church has probably been in operation for a long time before they arrived. When they come down there, however, quite often the white church tends to want to take over. It does not work that way. A partnership needs to be an equal, full-fledged partnership. As a matter of fact, if anyone takes the lead in urban/suburban partnership ministries, it should be the urban church because they know what the needs are as well as what the difficulties are.

The urban church, therefore, is the one to provide the input on culture and identify the highest priority needs. As an outsider, I do not understand the culture. I do not understand their needs, their resources. If I come in and try to impose something from a preconceived idea, it is quite likely to fail.

And vicè versà. If an urban church wants to partner in suburban ministry, the suburban church has to tell them how things work on their turf.

When I go downtown, it is the same as when a missionary goes overseas. As I said earlier, the missionary gets with the people of the area and asks how things work around there. What is taboo? What helps? What does not help? I need to find out where my efforts would be more likely to be spent wisely.

To minimize the possibility of destroying the relationship and its potential, the urban church may need to reach deep into its arsenal of Christian communication techniques to let the suburban church know when they are being heavy-handed and doing the control thing.

The Partnership Committee

The key to this whole thing is the partnership committee which does the groundwork. The suburban members of the committee should be people who are interested and have a heart for the partnership, not people who are coming in with a certain agenda and preconceived notions regarding how to solve the problems. They have to be people who can deal honestly, people the pastor and the board of elders can trust. The same is true of the committee members from the urban church.

The committee does the spadework up front. They need to be open and honest with one another. They should not offend one another thoughtlessly; but they should say, as lovingly as they can, "Listen, brother, this is what you are doing."

Not only does there have to be an understanding that we are going to be open and honest; but whenever a correction is needed, we must be willing to stop the program until the correction is made. Do not keep pressing on. Wait until the committee comes to a workable understanding.

Thirdly, there must be an ongoing, growing, personal relationship between the pastors of the two churches. They cannot be divorced from this whole process. There has to be an understanding at the top.

This committee is usually a subcommittee of the missions committee. In some churches, it is a separate committee. It is worthy of being a separate committee with a separate budget of its own. If you do not have that understanding up front, it will not work. What I would do in that committee is discuss how there is a tendency for the suburban church to take control. Quite often, the white church will come in with more organizational expertise in the persons of lawyers and businessmen and similar high-powered types. They will be accustomed to being in charge. It is only natural that they will attempt to impose their expertise onto the urban church.

In fact, the partnership should understand that even when things are not being done as efficiently as some would like, they may be effective on a relational level. I recognize that efficiency is important. So is stewardship. However, the relationship is more important than efficiency and effectiveness.

That is tough for white, middle-class, managerial-style persons because they are used to thinking about optimizing productivity and profit. They are in the partnership to use their gifts to make things happen. There has to be respect without condescension. Any member of the committee has to be able to tell another member, "You are being condescending."

If I am the one addressed by this statement, I have to be able to say, "Tell me how." It quite often happens that one brother will assume that the other brother is being condescending when that is not the case. What does it say in 1 Corinthians 13? Part of being loving is that I believe all things – I assume the other person is trying to be open and honest. By the way, if they are not open and honest – if they are there to ease a guilt or conscience – they do not need to be on that committee. People are giving their souls on the committee. They are opening up to all kinds of risk. It is going to take a lot to break down those barriers. Do not go into this coalition if your attitudinal emphasis is "They should be thankful to have my expertise."

Do Not Reinvent the Wheel. Life is too short; vital resources are too limited; and the need is too great. Try to capitalize on existing structures. Is there a coalition already in existence? Can a ministerial association be the basis for exploring urban/suburban cooperation? Check on those possibilities first. There are two things to watch out for in this context. If the association is vastly different from you theologically, you will have trouble plugging in. Or, if it is inflexible in its way of doing things, it is not going to really fit an urban/suburban partnership.

By the way, even if your city does not have a working partnership model, other cities do. Do the research. Check around; use the Internet. Call around and get resources. Talk to them and invest some time and energy. Ask them, *What have you had to work through?* Washington and Kehrein have a wonderful book entitled *Breaking Down Walls* which addresses the stuff they had to work through, such as what they were assuming the other was not doing, the element of time, the element of preaching style, and more. All of this needs to be worked through. There needs to be tolerance and understanding.

Usually a relationship partnership is a long-term commitment. What you do to get into that partnership is short-term projects together to see how it works out. The pilot program is a period of time dedicated to seeing if this is what we really want to commit to.

Education. If you plan to develop a cooperative relationship, research the issues first. Educate the church board and the congregation. You should not enter a partnership unless the church is in agreement with you. This process itself is going to take time. Let me tell you the steps I have taken in our church.

In the first place, I had to educate myself. The pastor has to be on board. In the second place, I taught and preached on the subject. In fact, I continue to do so. I bring the matter before the board constantly. I do not ramrod it, however. There are some old-time Anglos in our congregation, some of whom had businesses downtown which were burned out during the 1968 riots. That is a lot to overcome. Therefore, I work at the idea slowly, but surely. Sometimes I will say things like, "Does it make sense that we support missionaries in Mali and the Congo, but we will not go across the line in D.C. and be missionaries ourselves to our own city? It is some-what difficult to justify, isn't it?"

Education of the congregation is also a necessity. If only a small segment considers the partnership as their thing, it will not be successful. Partnership involves many sacrifices. So make sure the research and the education are done.

Promotion. Begin to have other people come up and talk about the idea. What you are looking for is somebody who will say, "Yes, that would be good to do." Do not begin by talking about the partnership and its commitments in broad and massive terms. That is not where people are going to start. Look for a project to be your test case.

For example, with us it was the Camp Bennett project. We were going to conduct a week of camp for inner-city youth. That was very successful. Then our people were interested in moving to the next level.

Be realistic about your expectations and the potential problems. Assemble a group of key people who are interested in this effort and take them down to see some inner-city ministries. For example, we go down to Central Union Mission – our equivalent to Pacific Garden Mission – and minister among them. There are also soup kitchens and clothing drives. Go down there and see what it is. What is in your mind may not be what it is like down in the city. Go down and visit and look around. We are not even talking about partnerships here. We are just going down to experience the city as it really is.

Meet with other churches downtown. Find out what they are doing. There might be some people already involved in reconciliation. Talk to them.

I spent nine months sitting in on the Fourth Presbyterian Inner-city Task Force meetings before we did anything at our church. Every Saturday I would drive all the way around the beltway – about a 45-minute trip. On the second Saturday of the month, I would meet with the committee, listening to what they were doing. Here I was, this fundamentalist, dispensationalist coming in to this reformed church, listening to what they were talking about, talking to their men, and finding out what is going on. You do not have to re-invent the wheel.

Again, I would recommend Raleigh Washington and Glen Kehrein's book on *Breaking Down Walls* as part of your research into what is already being done. Remember, however, that what they have done has been done over a long period of time. You cannot start where they are right now.

After proper research, exposure, and sensitization, begin seeking likely churches with which to partner.

Now, here is the key decision. Almost all of the time, the inner-city church is going to have a different worship style than the suburban white church. In fact, the more traditional the suburban white church, the more the difference is going to be. Secondly, your board, your committee, and your church have to decide the theological and ecclesiological boundaries with which they would be comfortable. If you are looking for a church just like yours in the inner city, you are going to have to go plant one. I mean, if you are a fundamental, non-charismatic church, are you comfortable partnering with a Pentecostal-style Baptist church in the city? You have to decide. Once you get into the partnership, there is a lot of damage if you are not comfortable with where they are. Obviously, they have to be born-again, evangelical people. However, their worship style might still be different than yours. If they are in a denomination or a fellowship, you have to understand their associations and their comfort zones. Therefore, you might have to search for a long time. You might talk to many different people. Do not jump into a partnership. Make sure all of the spadework is done up front.

You have been meeting with the inner-city task force in your church. When you begin to discern a possible partner church, this task force needs to plan a field trip to this potential partner, not to form the association, but to explore the possibility of one. Provide an opportunity for them to meet your church and your church to meet them.

The first several meetings should be exploratory. What are your respective doctrines? What are your practices? Are you compatible on essentials? Get to know them. Let them get to know you. Lay the groundwork so that when the task force presents the project to the board, there will be no question about their theology, their practice, and their ecclesiology. Furthermore, the task force should be prepared to answer whether and why you are comfortable with their expression of faith.

The Partnership Document

Prepare a document of understandings and expectations. That document will include the proposed partnership's philosophy, statement of faith, goals, objectives, and how you will work together. As an example, the document might contain language like,

> This committee derives its authority from the church board of Suburban Baptist Church and the board of Urban Baptist Church. This committee will function within the following guidelines, and the task force must be unanimous in their decision before they move forward.

You might feel that unanimous decisions are extremely difficult and, consequently, prefer to postpone the project. The truth of the matter is it is a lot of work. You are not dealing with one church. You are not dealing with one culture. Everybody must be comfortable with what is going on. Whatever language you decide on, the partnership must follow the guidelines meticulously. After the partnership is formed, schedule a kick-off banquet where the congregations celebrate their commitment to the partnership.

The two pastors and the boards must understand one another, make the commitment, and agree on a mode of working through misunderstandings. For example, Fourth Presbyterian found out several things in their partnership. Number one, the urban church's sense of time is different than theirs.

Fourth Presbyterian's committee members consisted of upper middle-class businessmen, one of whom is a lawyer for a major State Department bureau. When they say 10 o'clock in their organizations, things happen on time and not one minute after. They had to learn it does not work that way everywhere. They also found that there was a difference in understanding everyday language. They might say, *For us to work in your soup kitchen, you need to fix the sink.* The inner city church might agree that they will get that done this week. However, *this* week might not mean *this* week. It might mean some *future* week, which becomes *this* week someday. The sink may not be a priority to them.

The white church may have, for example, a lot of funds; and they will have an organization chart. Everything is done by committee. You would expect that it would be clear who is accountable and what the procedures are. You would expect that they would have forms for all of this stuff, right? After all, we are in a governmental city.

However, the black church gets involved in many different ministries. Their management style involves moving back and forth in a what-I-am-pulled-to-at-this-moment type of thing. If we say we are going to conduct a clothing drive between 8 and 12 on Saturday morning, that drive might actually happen between 11 and 4.

A real example of a wide variance in expectations involved the van. The van was going to be available during the clothing drive, but one of the sisters had to take the choir to some event. Now, *that* can be a very frustrating thing. I have been in committee meetings where the task force from the other church never showed up. Do you know what you do with that? You work *through* it. You *love* your brother.

The frustration can be mutual. The inner city Christians may feel, *You guys are so demanding. You want this and you want that, and you want it to work like clockwork. We have learned that emergencies cannot be scheduled. Chill out would you? Quit leaning on us.* Let me tell you something else. Be determined to bounce back.

It is important to set up a financial resource statement in this committee. There is the tendency for an urban church to think, *They have big money out there. They are our cash flow source.* For the urban church's sake, you cannot make them dependent. However, it is reasonable to anticipate that usually there will be more of an investment from the suburban church because they do have resources.

The other problem, mentioned above, is the white church has a tendency to come in saying, *We have the organization, and we will just run this thing.* However, the urban church will ask, *Why? Are we stepchildren?*

I spoke with an inner city leader who said, *The suburban church came down and just took over.* That is why sensitivity has to be worked at in this committee. It takes time. You might want to get the job done faster. Do not rush it, however. Make sure all the pieces are in place before you move on. Make sure the relationships are there. This is similar to what happens in a marriage, where you learn "party manners" before you get married; then all of a sudden you find reality on the honeymoon. Get past the party manners and get to know one another before expecting to make significant progress.

Be determined to be flexible and to show appreciation. When I go down to do a pulpit exchange, my preaching in the urban church is going to sound more systematic, more expository. On the other hand, my people have to understand that when we have a visiting urban black church, there is going to be a lot of zeal and light and heat and feeling in that sermon. Their music is going to sway more. It is going to incorporate more jazz and rhythm & blues styles.

Some of the partnerships are amazing. I have observed a partnership between an Episcopal church and a "Baptist-costal" church downtown. The Episcopal choir takes its turn, singing in an operatic style. Then the "Baptist-costal" choir expresses itself with finger snapping, swaying, and a lot of nonverbal going on. However, they have learned to appreciate one another in the Body of Christ. That is where education of your congregation comes in. You have to teach them to appreciate one another before the partnership begins.

Caveats

Some warnings are in order. Keep meticulous records on what was decided, what was done, who was supposed to do it, why, and when. Accountability and audit-ability are tremendously important. There is nothing more frustrating than, for example, one church telling the other church *we are going to do something*, and they do not do it. Keep the communication lines open. Never give up on that.

Secondly, do not enter a partnership where one church is disproportionately bigger than the other church. One will swallow up the other. You cannot have a suburban church of 400 going downtown to an urban church of 2000, and have the partnership work well. It will not.

Also, do not partner with a church that has many internal problems because you are not going to accomplish anything. The partnership will just get swallowed up in the other church's internal problems.

All churches have problems. Warren Weirsbe says, "Do you know what you call a church that has no problems? A dead church." That is exactly right. Living churches have problems. For example, there is a church up the street from us. We sold them our old building, and now they are in financial bankruptcy with all that that entails. If you wanted to consider working with them, you need to be aware that they cannot concentrate on a partnership because they are absorbed concentrating on the problems they have within their church.

Do not partnership with a church that is so radically different theologically or philosophically that you are going to have to spend all your time trying to develop a working agreement. There has to be some kind of agreement. It might not be totally perfect in every respect. However, they must be in fairly close agreement with you theologically.

Then if you indeed get into a situation where you are somewhat successful, start bringing in other churches. The suburban and the urban churches should both feel free to share with others, "This has been a really fantastic experience for my people. Why don't you come to our next meeting?" Invite another pastor or associate pastor to come and see what is happening. In that way, you begin to help other churches to see what is possible. Do not try to pressure them to make any commitments. However, if you begin to sense an interest there, then you may form an association.

Then, if your association begins to work, then you can approach the Hispanic churches, the Korean churches, and others. According to Arturo Lucero, there is a whole subset of Hispanic churches which hold separate Hispanic church meetings in Anglo church buildings for people who do not speak English. However, eventually you would like to see that begin to break down to where you could have more of a mixed congregation.

There can be integrated churches that are segregated within their memberships. Let me explain. Let's say 400 people come to church. Say there are 75 blacks and maybe 50 Hispanics. There is a tendency for the blacks to cluster with blacks and Hispanics with Hispanics. They just co-exist within the same building. If this is true of your congregation, address it before you end up exporting it to your partnership.

There are several ways to counteract this human tendency. We used to have fellowship dinners for circles of eights where some people signed up as hosts and some as guests. We arbitrarily divided the congregation for these dinners. So there might be a black family over here with a white family and a Hispanic family and another white family. This way people were provided the opportunity to get to know one another. We repeated this type of thing quarterly to encourage the mixing.

We have something special in our church. Maybe other churches do, too. I find it fascinating. We are very conscientious about making everybody feel welcome. As a result, perhaps, we have attracted a good number of mixed-race married couples. In our church of 200 people, we have about eight mixed-race married couples. When I talk to them, they say they feel comfortable in our church. We treat them just like any other couple.

We do not patronize them like, "Oh, we really want you here." However, we are also not standoffish. As Hamm says, there are different ethnic groups, but one human race. By the way, the mixed couples are a lot easier to mix in than the couples that segregate. The bottom line is you need to make it happen in your church before you export it to other churches.

Amos 3:3 asks, "Can two walk together except they agree?" There needs to be an understanding that there will be difficulties and it will take time, resources, and energy. This is one of the areas where we have run into many problems over the years. Our church was swept up in the 70s when Christian schools were being established all over. We established a school too, but had no concept of the time and energy a Christian school takes.

The same thing is true with a church partnership; it is going to take time, energy, and resources. We have to understand that the partnership may take resources away from some of the other things that the church was doing. The whole church has to make the commitment that this is worthwhile and it is what God has called us to do. When people start complaining, keep reminding them of that commitment.

Keep reminding them that this is a sacrifice and that in every new movement the first people to step forward are the ones who take the hits. I do not care if it is a George Washington Carver, a Booker T. Washington, or a Dr. Martin Luther King. If they take the lead, they are going to take some hits. However, their sacrifice is going to pave the way for others.

Everybody wants everybody else to do that and then they will jump on board, but somebody has to step forward. If God is calling you, take the hits as the Spirit leads each step.

An individual reminded me of Paul's writing from prison where he says "Rejoice" in Philippians. Because of the way Paul responded to adversity, many others were motivated to witness to the life-saving message of the Gospel, some even for spite. Paul took the hits. Even when some preached Christ out of envy and strife, it did not bother him, as long as the Word got out.

Puzzling. You may be just a little corner piece of the puzzle. However, if your corner piece were not there, the rest could not happen. There is a lot of talk about reconciliation with very little that is really actually being done. Someone once said, "After everything is said and done, there is a lot more said than done."

I do not wish to be anti-anybody, but Promise Keepers has married denominational and racial reconciliation when they really are separate issues. If I try to do racial reconciliation with a denominational church with which I do not agree theologically, I am going to kill the racial reconciliation issue. We must separate those two issues because one is based on a Biblical mandate. The other is based upon procedures of man. And they do not go together.

I am crying out for another thing. The government has done a lot to help the urban poor, but they have also enslaved them. They have given them a minimum of assistance without giving them any training or opportunity to get out of their situation. That is where the Church can contribute. Free up the Church to do that job.

Another point is that political correctness is killing us. Not everything in our culture is right! You know homosexual practice is not right. Fornication is not right. We must be free to dialogue honestly with one another and say such and such might be part of your culture; but it is not right. Likewise, I need to be open to receiving your rebuke that such and such is part of my culture but it is not right. Let's find a Biblical culture and get rid of those things that are not right. Tolerance of culture is not a Biblical mandate. Tolerance of people is, not culture.

Carver Bible College was established by the Independent Fundamental Churches of America (IFCA). So I asked one of the leaders why don't we have brother Randolph as a keynote speaker at our national convention? He said, "We have to be concerned about backlashes."

Backlashes? I thought we had come farther than that. That old timer is holding onto things. I said, "You have got to be kidding? We have to be concerned about what the Lord Jesus Christ thinks." We have a lot of work to do. We have to keep pressing forward.

Your foundational partnership document should address how you approach differences. If differences cannot be laid aside as secondary issues, then the partnership cannot be successful. Let me give you an example, and I am going to be very blunt here. Many Pentecostal churches cannot divorce evangelism from signs and wonders. Therefore, a fundamental Baptist church cannot form a partnership with them if they cannot lay that aside. Other non-doctrinal matters may be laid aside, however.

Sometimes the problem is not even in evangelism; it may get into the level of discipleship. I have to be comfortable as a suburban church that we are going to do evangelism and social action together. We will look to the urban church to disciple the people. The suburban church cannot expect to change the doctrine of the urban church. If I demand to do that, I cannot form a partnership. How we handle that has to be in the document.

Now, let's say we write into the partnership document that we agree on thus and so. That means we have run the language past our respective pastors, boards, partnership committees, and church members. All must agree that the defined issues are laid aside and will not become sources of disagreement. When one does become an issue, we go back to the document and say, *Wait a minute. We said this would not become an issue;* and we back away from it. This should not be construed to suggest that we should compromise essential articles of faith. It is better not to form a partnership than to lay aside something critical.

Let me give an illustration of this point. When I do pre-marital counseling, I try to identify issues that are potentially divisive, issues the engaged couple may try to sweep under the rug before the ceremony. I tell them that some of these issues will kill their marriage before it gets off the ground. Therefore, if they recognize that they cannot lay an issue aside permanently, the marriage should not happen until that problem is worked through. Minor things can become major things. If you are not comfortable with the other church's stand on a major issue, do not step into the partnership until the matter is resolved. There is no absolute timetable on this thing. It is unrealistic, however, to think that you will be able to resolve 100 percent of the disagreements.

If you are unable to work out a major conflict, back away from the partnership until it is resolved. Let's say you are moving forward in a partnership and a tough issue comes up. Suggest to the others that the partnership suspend what you are doing until you work through the matter. That is what that committee is there for. Then it has to report back to the boards.

If you have large churches involved, the partner-ship committee may have to report to an inner-city task force committee that reports to the missions

committee, which reports to the session, which reports to the elders, which reports to the pastor.
Why Are We Here? Motive is important as we contemplate partnering together. Your churches may be in sync theologically. They may have an understanding on how they worship and all of the other things mentioned above. We still need to ask why we are coming to the table together.

In places like Indianapolis, the government is giving monies to ministries that will partner with one another. Partnering has real value. Nonetheless, if money is the motivation for an urban/suburban partnership, it is not likely to work. Reality will hit after you receive the grant and then find yourself dealing with the everyday problems that seem to be compounded when you deal with them downtown. Then all of a sudden, that money will not look so good. Definition of motive has to be part of the partnership agreement. It would be the heartbreak of the missions society to send out people that – after three or four months on the field – decide they are *uncalled* from the field because they had not counted the cost. Luke 14 should be the hallmark chapter for the partnership committee.

Models

We will discuss three models. The first model is where the urban church and the suburban church are two **independent, self-supporting churches** coming together to partnership in the city. There is not a need from the urban church or suburban church for life support to be plugged in.

Another model is the **church plant model** where there is a mother church and a church plant that needs infusion of resources and energy in an effort to become a self-sustaining church. This is a different model which requires a different relationship. The partnership document is the resources port into this plant to get it to this point without expecting anything in return.

The third model is the **missions model**, where you have several churches, like on the mission field, investing resources into a mission church for the purpose of getting it to the point of self-sufficiency. One caveat to be aware of is the natural tendency to link power and control to the source of money. There has to be an understanding that that is not going to happen.

Sometimes when volunteers come from the mother church to work in the church plant, they come with a lordship philosophy, "*We* know how to put it on the next level." Sometimes they create a problem by just giving everybody everything. The congregation sometimes does not know how much money it costs to keep the doors open. In such a situation, the church plant and the people ministered to by the partnership will have no appreciation for the suburban church's generosity. Money must not be funneled down and given out without accountability. We call that the **government model** (the welfare level). That is enslavement. It creates a dependency to hand outs. It is condescending. It is patronizing.

The other level – the **helps** level – involves getting the urban church to become self-supporting and independent. This is the "growing child" level. The first model, by the way, is the old style missions model, where the missionary does everything in the field and keeps the mission church enslaved. The second model is the new model where we are trying to get indigenous churches to be self-sufficient.

The helps model is reminiscent of how George Washington Carver got his people out of a slavery mentality and, instead of growing cotton, got them growing peanuts and sweet potatoes. Booker T. Washington did the same thing at Tuskegee Institute. Sometimes a dependent church may have to take the initiative and go back to the mother church and say we have to sit down with a task force and re-draw our agreement to help us get to the point where we can learn to become self-sufficient. If the urban church is always the "baby," that church will never be self-sufficient. They have to learn to do it on their own. It is much easier to accept the handout than it is to grow, but Christ wants us to grow churches.

7 – Struggles and Solutions in the Area of Racial Reconciliation

[Dr. Paul Dixon presented his views at the third Multiracial Ministry Conference. This chapter is an edited transcript of Dr. Dixon's comments as well as some interactions he had with seminar participants.]

I am not an expert on what it means to struggle in the area of racial reconciliation, nor do I claim that I have accomplished much in the area. However, as an evangelist, I have to declare that I have been committed to racial reconciliation ever since I received Jesus as my personal Savior. After all, 2 Corinthians 5 tells us that we are ministers of reconciliation. However, it is clear to me that even with that explicit Scriptural injunction concerning reconciliation, including racial reconciliation, we

---

[1] Dr. Paul H. Dixon is in his 23rd year as president of Cedarville College, a Christian college in southwest Ohio. Prior to his ministry as president, he served the Lord for 14 years as an evangelist.

continue to have struggles in our churches, struggles in our colleges, and struggles in our homes.

Struggles and Solutions in Our Churches

The majority of this chapter deals with struggles and solutions in our churches. I believe Martin Luther King, Jr., put his finger on the nerve of the issue when he said "The most segregated hour in America is 11 o'clock on Sunday morning." Fortunately, over the last thirty years there have developed some successful efforts of integrating the Church. Let me set the stage by identifying some models and some of the differences of opinion on this topic.

First Baptist Church of Willingboro, New Jersey, one of the most successful integrated churches that I have ever been in, was planted when I was still an evangelist. A Cedarville College graduate will soon become an assistant pastor in that church. He is black and the pastor is white. This church is approximately 50 percent black and 50 percent white. It has been that way for as long as I can remember. There are several things that have worked together to contribute to this success.

Shared Leadership. For one thing, the church's community is similarly 50 percent black and 50 percent white. Willingboro is remarkable in that it is a very prosperous community with not only a large number of middle-class whites and black, but also a high percentage of upper middle-class white and black families. When you go to that church, you do not sense tensions. Part of the reason is that there is shared leadership both at the board level and on the pastoral staff.

Consistent Bible Preaching. Secondly, there is consistent Bible preaching with strong doctrinal content at this church. It has always been a strong Biblically committed church. It is really wonderful to go into that church and to become immersed in the worship that takes place. There is love and respect for everyone in the church. They also respect others outside of their community.

Not only is their success related to their economic equality, but there is also a measure of educational equality. Most of these people are college graduates. So on the one hand, I hold it up as the most successful model of racial integration with which I have ever been associated. Yet, on the other hand, First Baptist does not reflect a lot of communities in terms of their educational and economical equality.

I have been a college president for 22 years. For 14 year before I became president at Cedarville, I was a full-time evangelist. In fact, I was an evangelist all the way through college and seminary. In essence, I have 42 years of itinerant ministry. As an itinerant minister, I can attest to the fact that the vast majority of the churches I have been in do not make an effort at bringing minorities into the church. Of those who do, I find few which are successful. There are notable exceptions. Unfortunately, however, too many spend a lot of time trying to get it done and do not pull it off.

Another thing we are wrestling with is the fact that some members of the minority community do not want to be a part of an integrated church. I speak at some really outstanding black churches. There are very few white faces in some of those congregations. Most of those black people do not want to be in any other church. Frankly, they want the evangelism, the discipleship, and the reaching out that takes place to take place within their church.

Let me tell you about a church right now that is just blowing some of us away. A good friend of mine, a black minister, pastors a church in the Midwest. A nearby white church has had some major problems, and many of their people are seeking other places to worship. As a result, this black church has had an influx of whites coming to the church. In fact, there are probably more whites attending that church than most formerly all-black churches that I know. In spite of what many of us would classify as a moving of the Lord, my friend made the following observation:

> I cannot believe how racist my people are. They just do not like all of these white people being in "our" church. I am having major leadership problems trying to figure out what to do. Some of the people are accusing me of playing up to the white people because they give more money. Some of them are saying I am changing the music style for the white folks' sake, and all kinds of similar complaints.

Another illustration of the struggles that go on was related to me by Pastor Eddie Dobson, a good friend of mine at Calvary Undenominational Church in Grand Rapids. Eddie, a white pastor, has a heart for all people. He has really reached out to the minorities in Grand Rapids. Eddie related a meeting he had with a major black leader who has a very large congregation in Grand Rapids. The pastor said to Eddie,

Look, I want to be your friend; but I do not want my church integrated; and I do not want your church integrated. Our people really are going to fit better in our church; and your people are going to fit better in your church. I do not want to be a part of anything like that [referring to integrated congregations].

Again, it appears that there are elements within the black community that are more devoted to that approach than to the idea of trying to integrate things and trying to have a ministry regardless of color.

An Issue of the Heart. (*Editors' Note:* What follows are some of the interactions of Dr. Dixon with the observations and concerns of clergy and lay leaders at the conference who were concerned about the struggle toward racial reconciliation. This first vignette from a seminar participant highlights an essential ingredient for successful racial reconciliation.)

PARTICIPANT: [In order for racial reconciliation to work,] we have to start with our hearts first. As a child, I grew up in a black church, but we also visited the neighboring churches that were white. My family had no problems with it because we were brought up as Christians. Christians ... are supposed to love everyone.... Because of the situation I was in as a child, I fellowshipped with white brothers and sisters. However, nowadays blacks are said to have a different cultural background. The music is different. The preaching is different. The praise is different. Everything is different. Really, truthfully, I do not feel that.

We have some white brothers and sisters who have joined because they are comfortable in our church. I have not experienced any attitudes like, "We do not want you here." I do not feel that way and my black brothers and sisters do not feel that way....

Don Bartlette explained how he had been rejected by the white race – it is the same thing with the black race. We have been rejected by the white race. It goes right back to the heart. If we know Jesus Christ, we know who He was; and we know who He is. If He lives in our hearts, our hearts can be changed and we will not discriminate because of color. However, we can break that barrier only with our hearts.

Even though there may be many differences in terms of our cultural backgrounds, we can still mingle together and be a unit. But are we willing to do that? It takes all of us to do it. It is not going to come overnight. It is a growing process.

If you ask almost anybody if they want to go to heaven, they will answer yes.... Well then, they are going to see all kinds of races there.

Dr. Dixon: I would agree that racial reconciliation is a heart issue. Meaningful change takes time. Racial reconciliation requires persistent commitment to a process. We need to be alert to what is going on around us.

Simultaneous, But Unrelated, Changes. [Another participant related how racial reconciliation began at her congregation at the same time that changes were being made to the worship schedule.]

PARTICIPANT 2: I have been very concerned about what I have seen at our church. We have acquired a lot of whites in the past couple of years – approximately 5 percent of our church attendance. (Of an attendance of 7500, you are talking somewhere in the neighborhood of 400 people.) We have begun having three services on

Sunday morning. We do not have evening church. Our pastor preaches the Word.

Dr. Dixon: A lot of the churches on the West Coast do not have Sunday night services any more. They devote all of their energies to Sunday mornings.

PARTICIPANT 2: The Caucasians who have come to our church have not accepted, or cannot get used to, things such as the theme of the praise. They come only to hear the Word. Perhaps that is why they have joined the church.

However, once the preaching is done, ... they leave right away.... They go on home instead of getting involved personally with other people. What I would like to see is the children going to activities and the adults becoming members of the choir, the usher board, and things like that where you can really see that we are together as one. However, there is still that segregation there without a doubt; and that is kind of odd because the Word is being preached and they love that.

Dr. Dixon: Of course, that happens a lot in the Caucasian church, too. A high percentage of people who just come in there to kind of take, but they do not really get involved in the church or in people's lives.

PARTICIPANT 3: In addition, there could be fear of rejection. We come to church to hear the Word so we can apply it to our lives so we can live better outside the church. However, sometimes we fear to mingle because of our past. In many cases, there is a lot of animosity still within us, consciously or subconsciously, because of what went on years ago, although many of us are trying to come together.

The Chicago Experience.

PARTICIPANT 4: My wife and I live and work in the inner city of Chicago. We live in a predominantly non-white neighborhood. There was a time when we attended a predominantly black church that supported the youth ministry with which we work, but that was difficult. We enjoyed the worship, but we had a hard time connecting in that context.

There were other factors that made it difficult. The church, drew people from up to an hour away. The only time many of the people were together was Sunday morning. Many did not get together beyond that, or they got together where they lived. Over time, that became frustrating because we could never figure out how to connect with people from the church on a personal basis. We did not sense any hostility or anything like that.

Dr. Dixon: If you go back and look again at the church model discussed at the beginning of this chapter, you will begin to sense why it has been successful. Most of the members live in the same community. They probably work together. Their children go to school together. It is a lot easier to be successful in that context than it is in the Chicago situation just described.

Be aware. We are talking about somewhat isolated instances – what researchers refer to as anecdotal examples. We are glad for the success in various churches around the country. However, we cannot say whether their success can be duplicated somewhere else simply because the other place looks the same to the naked eye. In other words, we are not sure we know the answers that will make other churches successful in the area of multiracial ministry.

In spite of not knowing all the answers, we are still required to follow the Spirit as He leads us in our local setting. For example, the Brooklyn Tabernacle has done an amazing job of bringing together Hispanics, whites, African Americans, drug-addicts, alcoholics, rich people, young folk, you name it. They have built it on prayer; and, of course, people love their music.

Prayer – Indispensable.

PARTICIPANT 5: We attempt to do multiracial ministry on an outward level. People have to have a desire in their hearts to want to make a change. Someone has to step out. That is really what it is about in the Word. We need to go before God in prayer, and then we have to live the Word.

Dr. Dixon: Prayer is essential. The only way multiracial ministry is going to work is if God pulls it off. We are so wicked and depraved that there is no way we can do it on our own. With God's help, some amazing things can happen. We need to understand that and wait on God and see what He is going to do.

Respect.

PARTICIPANT 6: There is a white couple at our church. They say the Lord led them there. The husband is very advanced in sign language, so he teaches a signing class. They were prayerful about it. And they have probably gone through times of denial and neglect or whatever, but now they are fitting in. The wife is in our ladies' class. She makes herself available.

Dr. Dixon: If you are going to have a relationship with people, you have to work at it. One problem with white middle class Christians is that we have the tendency to go into situations and do all of the talking. A number of my pastor friends who happen to be black tell me that they have really appreciated that I call them up to ask for input on what I should do about various situations, and where I should place my emphasis. Some of them tell me that I am one of the first white men who has ever asked for their opinion on anything. If we want to have a relationship, we are going to have to learn from each other.

Godly Integration Starts Somewhere.

PARTICIPANT 7: The church in Baltimore where I was an assistant for ten years is probably one of the best examples I have seen of an integrated congregation. On Sunday morning, we would run about 1000 people. There would be approximately 50 percent white, 40 percent black, and 10 percent other. And I do mean other, although most of them were Chinese. We translated for them just like at the UN. We had a translator, and they had earphones.

It came to the point where we almost did not see ourselves as diverse. We thought that was just the way it was supposed to be. And people came in. The key that drew in the people was the consistent teaching of the Word of God. They were hungry for the Word. We crossed socioeconomic standards of status as well as racial barriers. Our people came from the inner city of Baltimore as well as from the upper middle-class area where our church was located. Various races and colors from all of those cross segments were there in the church.... The teamwork was incredible.

This is the church's 25th year. When Pastor Johnson started the church, a lady who attended the church up the street called and said, "I am black and they won't let me sing in the choir. If I come to your church, can I sing in the choir?"

He said, "Lady, I do not care if you are green. If you love the Lord Jesus you can sing here." That was the first family that came, and they have been there more than 20 years. The other church's loss was our gain. That was the start of something beautiful. And it was the result of Pastor Johnson's attitude that we are here to serve and to learn.

Dr. Dixon: That is great. That is a good model.

PARTICIPANT 8: I am trying to do that where I am now, but I am finding it hard. That one happened naturally, but it is going to take a while in our context –I have a changing community.

Dr. Dixon: As I recall, your community is changing to include Hispanics as well as blacks. It seems right that your core white group is trying to reach out.

Beyond Bible Study: An Effective Strategy.

PARTICIPANT 9: It seems to me that the solid Bible teaching referenced earlier is strategic to racial reconciliation. Yet, we have so many definitions of good Bible teaching. I do not think I have met a person who does not say that their church teaches the Bible and they would hate to leave. Yet we know there are different qualities of the way people and congregations live out what "thus saith the Lord."

While it still remains that we need good Bible teaching, we need to also focus on applying the Word. That may mean that the pastor needs to exert leadership by saying something to the effect that the people should plan intentionally for fellowship with each other outside the church walls. Our pastor in Los Angeles demonstrated how effective this could be. He instructed us, "The host ought to have coffee and maybe dessert." He did not say, "Your host can't afford to prepare dinner for guests frequently." It was clear to me that in light of California's depressed economy at the time, many in our number could not afford to have people over for dinner. However, having them over for coffee was far less of a burden.

That seemed to liberate many people. A lot more activities were planned since we were not expected to spend a lot of money in order to be a host or hostess. With leadership signaling that this is what needs to be done, people are more likely to follow in the long run than to have some of us lay people get the bright idea and start it. Sure, that can work, but bottom-up does not seem to be as effective as top-down.

Dr. Dixon: One thing we have to recognize is that a lot has to do with your community – where you are, and what is going on there. For instance, we have 2500 people who live in Cedarville. We have a black contingency in Cedarville. From what I can tell, we have a pretty good black church there. My pastor, David Graham, is one of the warmest human beings you would ever want to meet. We have a big Labor Day deal that goes on at the park in Cedarville. At the same time, we are doing our thing, the black people get together across the creek and do their thing.

Well, our pastor David Graham started showing up at their thing. And they just love it. They think it is great that David comes in there and eats with them and just fellowships with them. Many unsaved people come to that event. This is not a church thing that they are doing; it is just a community thing. God has given him a ministry in lives. The black pastors and he are also good friends.

Are we to say that because David has not reached out and brought a lot of blacks into our congregation that he is not successful in communicating cross-culturally? I do not think so. We have to be careful that we do not stereotype what success is. There are a lot of different communities and a lot of different people that contribute to that. As we have touched on before, it has to do with our heart.

Struggles and Solutions in our Homes.

I want to move on quickly to the struggles and solutions in our homes. Most of our homes have a lack of exposure to other races and cultures. We have to figure out how to bring our kids into that world. We have to do things intentionally: (1) Be intentional. (2) Have a plan.

I am big on strategic planning and strategic thinking. So, what is our strategic plan for introducing our kids to other cultures? We can use films. We can use videos. We can take them on inner-city missions trips. When my son was a youth pastor in Michigan, he took his youth group to an inner city for ministry every summer. They went to Chicago. He took them to Los Angeles. He took them to New York City where they worked among Chinese people. Every time he took his youth group on these ministries, he took his own children with him, too. They had an exposure to other cultures by going on these mission trips. I think we need to strategize in our families how we can get exposure for our children and our grandchildren.

A Systems Approach. When God's people convene to work on issues and opportunities, it is often amazing what develops. One seminar participant opened up a discussion on the need to give minority students full access to American educational institutions. At the risk of oversimplification, let me preface the discussion by stating the issue as succinctly as I can.

Minorities, particularly African Americans, want equal access to higher education in America. Some whites respond by asking that everyone compete on an equal footing for the limited number of openings at the best professional schools. Some African Americans – not all – respond that they have been denied equal opportunity to learn to compete on standardized tests and similar admission criteria. They feel, therefore, that they deserve some appropriate gesture of good will to help compensate for the barriers that have been thrown in their way historically. It may take one wiser than Solomon to find a middle ground capable of satisfying both sides of this issue. In the meantime, here is some of the enlightened thinking that was put forth at the conference:

PARTICIPANT: One needs to take a systems approach to such problems and not rely on a simplistic, "Do not lower your standards" retort. There is more to it than that. Of course, we should not lower our standards. Of course, we should not introduce reverse discrimination. However, we dare not overlook the fact that a supposed emphasis on upholding "fair" entrance requirements essentially rubber stamps the unequal attainments foisted upon minorities historically and locks so many of them into future training opportunities which mitigate against their obtaining full participation in the economic and professional life of America.

At the same time, the educational system needs to develop some tutorial programs and other enriching experiences for students who need such. Further, the African American community needs to cooperate in supplying students who have a drive to achieve. The colleges could then request of that coalition, "Send us a certain number of students next year who will meet the existing standards for our institutions."

Perhaps the college community could provide some inputs to help prepare youth for success. I recall taking my tenth grade son to an information session at Purdue for aspiring engineers. Is that an idea whose time has come in the Christian college community?

The urban colleges would have greater access to high school students. Their interactions with high schoolers could benefit small-town colleges as well. By way of clarification, for example, Moody students and faculty could tutor Chicago high school students to groom them for that major transition to college.

Although our ministry is not a college, we are struggling with preparing teens for college in Highland Park, Michigan. Several of us who take Luke 14 seriously believe that we should have a tutorial program there as part of our Christian community development outreach.

Dr. Dixon: The suggestion may have some merit. I should point out, however, that it can be just as tough academically to go through the four-year program at Moody. We have young people at Cedarville who have also attended Moody. Both colleges have similar high standards.

One of the things that I have really been burdened for and had a vision for is doing some summer programs for high school students that could provide some mentoring and some tutoring for students at every level. We are really at the cutting edge of technology at Cedarville; so there is a whole lot we could teach high school kids about technology.

The Difficult Commandments. On another note, there is some interest in what Cedarville College teaches in the area of difficult commandments regarding racism. Frankly, there is not a course on the commandments. We do work on the issue in chapel.

Furthermore, for years we have observed Martin Luther King Day in chapel. I hope you understand that there are not many historic, fundamental, conservative, evangelical schools that are having Martin Luther King Days. I get up and talk about him and his work. I have preached on him. I have tried to be a student of Dr. King. I do not believe you can separate the civil rights movement in America from Martin Luther King, Jr. They just go together.

Struggles and Solutions in Our Colleges.

People often ask me if I ever have cross-cultural problems at Cedarville College. I tell them that when you have a president who is a sinner, and a vice-president who is a sinner, and 2500 students, and 150 full-time faculty who are sinners – you bet your life we have problems. Any time you put sinners together you are going to have problems.

We sometimes talk about the bad side of the college years; but I have seen some good things in Christian college kids. I will guarantee you that they did not arrive at a mature spiritual perspective from the short time they spent at Cedarville College. In most cases, they got it from things they had heard and observed in their homes.

Recruiting: Changing Paradigms. One participant rightly observed that some of the ways to get different groups of new students has to do with where we recruit. Cedarville, Ohio, is not exactly in that part of the country that draws a large minority contingency, especially Hispanics. If we target Hispanics, for example, it is really tough to be successful in our recruiting. But we have a plan where we work on different groups. We advertise in targeted publications. We have special leadership scholarships targeting different groups in an effort to get them to campus.

Someone suggested that if we look at a pie of where we recruit, that would give us some indication of why we receive the student mix that we do. It is not just the location of Cedarville. What we are seeing, however, is that nationally 80 percent of all students go to school within their own state. When you consider that about 35 percent of Cedarville students come from Ohio, we are obviously drawing very heavily from the border states, Michigan, Indiana, and Pennsylvania. Michigan is one of our largest states for students. We also get good response from New York, the New England states, and New Jersey.

PARTICIPANT 11: Is it reasonable to assume that allocating more resources in recruiting minorities might be productive? A specific target could lead to a plan for more aggressive minority recruitment. You would then know what areas you would have to target even within your own state. You might have to use as much as 50 percent of your recruiting resources to reach a goal of 10 percent minorities. We could talk about the science of integrating. If there is a desire to integrate an institution, you would have to go after the desired students. Otherwise, the dynamics that be are the dynamics that are going to govern.

Dr. Dixon: We have to operate like other schools in some respects. We devote a lot of energies where we are going to get the most return on our investment because we only have so many dollars. Higher educational institutions are really under the gun financially. There is no question about that. It is a constant challenge.

PARTICIPANT 12: We have found that urban extensions are very profitable for rural colleges, at least for Spring Arbor College in Michigan. In that concept you take the education to the people, and they can learn while they maintain their existing jobs. That may be something to consider.

Dr. Dixon: We have looked at that. We have pretty much a traditional residential campus, and we know that we cannot expect adult learners to drop their wives, jobs, and everything. So going out is possible. However, there is another distinction – we only accept the born-again student. If you look at most programs that Spring Arbor has helped to set up – they have helped a lot of schools set up other programs, and they generally broaden that enroll-ment. Adult learning tends to reach out to the non-Christian as well. We would have to make a major philosophical change for us to move in that direction. At this point, we have not been willing to make that change.

Wrap-Up. To wrap up, let me say that one of the new things that we have on the drawing board is a graduate school. We welcome all students to apply to that program. Secondly, with our advanced computer and telecommunications technology, we are going to be doing some pretty aggressive things in distance learning. What I hope is that we could bring some of our resources to your churches and provide some programs in Christian higher education that way.

Even though I was the resource person for the seminar, I saw myself more as a moderator. The many participants in the seminar were also authorities on interracial relationships in their own rights. I like the fact that whenever I meet with people interested in the topic, they tell me about developments that I never would have thought of. For example, some of the black churches in Cleveland, Ohio, have a way of fellowshipping together one Sunday night each month. Each of the churches in the fellowship agrees to dismiss their service; and they all go to the same church and worship and fellowship together.

We do not do this very much, but I think it is great that every once in a while I hear about a white church that invites an entire black church to come over for a Sunday night service – and vicè versà. The more we can do that; and the more the kids in our homes can be exposed to that, the more we are going to break down these barriers. We really should give kids a chance. They do not know that there is a color barrier unless, of course, we teach them that there is one.

8 – I Could Write a Book

Don Bartlette[1]

In a small community in North Dakota many, many years ago, there lived a Native American family. They lived up in the hills in a one-room log cabin. They lived in the hills because they were not welcome in that small community. In that small community in North Dakota there were seven churches. But my people were not welcome in those churches. My parents happened to be Native American people. My parents happened to be poor people. But they valued family. They wanted many, many children because that is important in our culture. My mother and father both came from large families. My mother is from a family of 15 children. My father comes from a family of 10.

Tragedy in the Hills

My father happened to be a tall man. He was a strong man. My father was an athlete, a runner, and a hunter. My father loved fishing; and my father wanted me, the first-born son, to be everything he was. As he helped my mother to bring me into the world in that

---

[1] Dr. Don Bartlette, a Native American, is founder of a travel ministry. A former social worker, counselor, and educator, Don is an author, a public speaker, and father of eight.

one-room shack, my father looked at me and then put me down. My father became very angry when he noticed three things that made me different. My father noticed I only had half a nose hanging on the left side of my face. My father noticed I had no upper lip. When my father looked for the third time, he noticed a huge hole in the top of my mouth.

My father was a proud man. He did not want a handicapped son. (What my family does not want me to disclose publicly is that my father began running away into a world we now call alcoholism, a world from which my father never came back.)

On the other hand, my mother – a beautiful, full-blooded Chippewa Native American woman, a woman who valued life, all life, a woman who valued family, a woman who valued children – hung on to me, wanting me. Not knowing what to do with a severely handicapped baby, she nevertheless valued me. As my mother hung onto me, my grandmother became frightened. She ran to that small white community where they had seven churches, looking for a doctor. When the doctor came up into the hills, when he saw I was handicapped, when he reflected that we were Native American people, he told my mother, "Send him away. He does not belong in our community. He will never speak. He will never learn. Send him away now."

Nevertheless, my mother would not send me away. She valued life. As she hung onto me, the doctor became angry. He went into that small community and told the people that I was a freak Indian baby. Out of their prejudice, they came up into the hills and, walking into our one-room shack, the people from that white community took me away from my mother. Not wanting a child like me in their community, they sent me away to another community.

However, the people there wouldn't have me either; so they put me in a hospital. Another doctor evaluated me. He must have been a man of compassion. He took the left part of my nose, and connected it to the right side of my face, leaving me with a very flat nose. For many, many years of my life, he continued to work on me. He pulled my upper lip together, but he knew not what to do with that hole in the top of my mouth.

That doctor believed that a Native American child ought to grow up in his natural environment. So he sent me back to live with my mother and father. For nine years, I was not allowed in the community. I was not allowed in the churches. I was not allowed in the public schools. For nine years, I grew up in a world of isolation, a world of hunger, a world of poverty, a world of alcoholism. That became for me a world of child abuse – nine years of wondering why I could not speak, wondering why my father drank heavily, wondering why he blamed my mother for my being handicapped, wondering why I was never allowed in the community.

Finding Food in a New World

In those nine years, as a member of a poor, isolated, lonely family, there were many times when I became very hungry. I remember being so hungry that I went down into that small community of seven churches, and there in an isolated area that they call the city dump, I found the white people throwing away food. Out of my hunger, I remember picking up the food and pushing it down that hole in my mouth because I had never been taught how to chew my food. As the food went down, the pain and hunger went away momentarily.

As I returned to the dump looking for more food, I found clothing. I also found written materials that fascinated me. As I took the materials home with me, my mother saw me wanting to read, wanting to learn, wanting to understand. One day my mother followed me to the dump. That was the day my mother became angry when she saw me playing with the rats, wanting to have real friends. She took me out of the dump and brought me to a parochial school run by a church. The church told my mother they would not allow me in their school because I could not talk and we were Native American people.

Learning to Hate in School

In her frustration, my mother took me to a public school and left me on the playground. The children in the public school came running toward me, looking at me, laughing at me, pointing fingers at my flat nose, calling me names like "smelly Indian." They took me by my hair, threw me against the building, kicked me, and hit me. One girl spit all over my face.

As they made fun of my alcoholic father, I ran into the school. The children followed me, poking me in the back with their pencils, tantalizing me, rejecting me, showing prejudice because I happened to be Native American. My first grade teacher locked me in a closet. My second grade teacher refused to teach me. My third grade teacher told the children that I was mentally retarded. When the children heard that, they took me up into the hills, tied me to a tree with my hands behind my back, and hit me in the face until the blood ran down on my shirt. They laughed at me and reminded me that I was an Indian. That hurt me on the inside. They left me tied to that tree for hours, late into the night. As a young Native American child, I began to hate my handicap. I began to hate my Native American heritage. In addition, I began to hate the white people in the world around me.

An old man found me and untied the rope and set me free. I ran home that night and encountered what those seven churches never knew because they never came into the hills. They never came into my home. They never came face to face with my family. As I arrived home that night, my alcoholic father happened to be drinking. When he saw the blood on my shirt, he became angry. My father took me and threw me into the wall, kicking me, hitting me, rejecting me.

I began to hate my alcoholic father. That night, as he hurt my mother, I ran into that small white community. I broke into the church looking for food, looking for shelter, wanting somebody to help me, wanting to be safe. I began to break into the white peoples' homes. I broke into the public school.

When they found me one morning sleeping under a teacher's desk, the police came for me. The policemen happened to be white. They happened to be prejudiced. The two officers put me in the trunk of their car to take me to the local jail. There they took me by my hair and called me a stinking Indian as they locked me in a cell. Late that night I saw the two policemen drinking.

Fear overwhelmed me as they unlocked my cell, held me by my hair, beat me, and humiliated me in unspeakable ways. As they threw me on the floor, I began to hate with a hate that I could not handle inside of me.

My father came after me the next morning. He had been drinking. In the privacy of our home, where the church never came, my father took me by my hair, and removed his large leather belt. As he hit me repeatedly in front of my mother, my father fell asleep from the alcohol. Out of hate within my heart, I crawled over near the window. There I took my father's rifle. As I prepared to kill my father, my mother, who valued life, took the rifle out of my hands. I did not kill my father, and I am glad today.

A Christian Woman's Touch

At that moment in my childhood, as a 12-year-old child, I may never have survived had it not been for one Christian woman from one of the seven churches in that small community. I want you to meet that woman. She was a prominent woman. She came from a wealthy family who owned property and a business. When this white woman heard we were Native American people, when she heard I was handicapped, when this woman found that we were living in a world of isolation, in a world of poverty, when she learned that I was not in school, that I could not talk, that my father was an alcoholic, she became concerned. It was out of her concern that she came into my life.

There were seven churches in our community. Yet, only one member of one church came into my world. I will never forget her. In *Macaroni at Midnight* I wrote about this prominent, wealthy woman who took me into her life, who welcomed me into her home, who put her hand on mine – not laughing at me, not rejecting me, not calling me a stinking Indian. Not hurting me, not showing any prejudice.

As she put her hand on mine, that became a moment of change in my world. A white person touching me, not hurting me, not rejecting me! With her hand on mine, telling me in a gentle voice, "I want to help you. I care about you," she took me into her life. It was that woman who put her hand into my mouth and taught me how to move my tongue, how to hold a fork, how to put the food between my teeth. At the age of 12, she taught me how to chew my food, how to read, and how to write. She taught me how to survive in a white man's world. She taught me how to take a shower, how to groom my hair, how to work to earn quarters so I could buy my own clothing. I could even buy toothpaste that my family had never been able to have.

It was the white woman who took me into her home, gave me food, and showed me love. She met my needs. She became an object of hate – even by her church. But she never gave in to their prejudice.

I will never forget how she touched me, encouraged me, loved me, taught me, accepted me, embraced me, and empowered me. It was incomprehensible that anybody white would care about me. They told her, "You're wasting your time; he'll never be able to talk." It was she with her patience who put a clothespin on my nose, and with a mirror under my nose, using a small radio and a tape recorder, taught me to make the air flow through my lips. This helped me learn to make sounds. Week after week, month after month, year after year, she helped me. I watched the community reject her, watched her church tell her not to bring me into the church. It was this white woman who one night, told me to return home to my parents.

It happened to be around the midnight hour. My mother had a hot bowl of macaroni waiting for me. That night in my home, I demonstrated what the white woman had taught me. In front of my parents, I picked up a fork. At midnight, as I put the macaroni between my teeth, my parents saw something they thought would never happen. I chewed my food. As my father watched me that night, I put my tongue in the right place; and then I made a sound.

As my parents heard me trying to speak, they decided to ask the white woman if she would help me more. It was that one white woman who took me to a large hospital. There, they gave me a new nose. They gave me a new upper lip. They gave me new teeth. They put a round steel plate in the top of my mouth. And, with the help of that woman, with the encouragement of that woman, with motivation from that woman, I went into a six-year program where I learned to speak as I now do.

The Power of One

When I returned home, I saw the woman had begun to have an impact on the community. When the churches saw the results of her loving me – touching me – they began changing. When the public school saw me learning from her, they began teaching me. The whole community began changing. One woman impacted an entire community when they saw her love for Native American people.

They saw us walking into her home. They saw her relating to my alcoholic father, showing him dignity and respect. As my father began changing, the community changed more. The church began changing. The school began changing. Through the help of that woman, I became the first handicapped Native American child to ever graduate from high school as Valedictorian of my class.

Why? More importantly than that, with my new speech, I asked the white woman one day, "Why do you touch me? Why do you hold me? Why do you feed me? Why do you teach me? Why do you welcome me into your home?"

Then she did what the seven churches never did. She showed me a book. As she opened the book, she began telling me about the Word of God. She began teaching me about a heavenly Father whose Son died even for me. I could not understand that from the white woman. I could not believe in a heavenly Father loving me when my own father never loved me. But, she opened the Word of God and taught me about love and forgiveness. She told me, "One day, I know, you'll want Jesus in your heart." I could not do it then. The hurt and the hate inside overwhelmed me. However, I never forgot that woman.

With her help, I became the only member of my family to ever go on to a university. I became a social worker, a counselor, and an educator. As I began working with minority children, hungry children, isolated children, lonely children all over America, I began running away from my Native American heritage. I began to pass for white, trying to hide my deficits. I never told anybody who I was or where I had come from. Nobody ever knew about the child Don Bartlette.

As I was working in Michigan 29 years ago, I met another white woman – a beautiful person, a person who valued all people. She accepted me for who I was. Unfortunately, I married her out of my hurt and out of my hate. My wife, who had grown up in the church, who came from a Christian family in Indiana, knew nothing about the child Don Bartlette when she married me. With some pain, my wife could reveal to you that for six long years I took the hurt and my hate for white people out on her and her family.

As I took her away from her family, I began noticing that my wife believed in the Bible. During those six years of pain, she never rejected me. She never showed hate for me. She tried to understand my hurt. It was only through the Word of God that my wife persevered. She invited me to a small evangelical church on Easter Sunday 1974. I did not want to go to a church. I had grown up hating the church. They were never there for me in my child-hood; but because of my wife's encouragement, I went to that church. They believed in the Word of God.

At that church, the people welcomed me, touched me, embraced me, showed love to me, and taught me about the Word of God. Through that small white evangelical church, I began understanding what the first white woman had taught me as a child. Therefore, it was that 26 years ago, through the ministry of that white evangelical church, I opened the Word of God, I opened my heart, and I invited Jesus Christ to become my Savior.

As I became a born-again believer, it was my wife and the Word of God who encouraged me to accept my disability, to relate to my Native American heritage, and then to go back to that small community. Through Luke 23:34 where Jesus said, "Father, forgive them, for they know not what they do," I learned to forgive the white people who had rejected me and hurt me. Then I relied on the combined power of Luke 23:34 and John 13:34, "A new commandment I give unto you, that you love one another, even as I have loved you," to go back to my father. For nine years, before he died, I was able through the power of Jesus Christ to forgive my father, to love my father, and then to lead my father to Christ.

I still remember the white woman, the only one from those seven churches who took the risk of touching me, encouraging me, loving me, believing in me, accepting me, and teaching me the Word of God. Now, through the power of Jesus Christ, I can tell you I no longer hide the disability. I no longer hate my Native American heritage. Most important of all, I no longer hate white people. I challenge you to look within your heart as well and then to touch the need within all people.

As I close, I want to share from Matthew 28:19, where we are told,

> Go, therefore, and make disciples of ALL nations, baptizing them in the name of the Father and the Son and the Holy Spirit. Teaching ALL of them to observe ALL that I have commanded you.

Please bow your hearts and pray with me a prayer that I am not ashamed to pray:

> Heavenly Father, Lord Jesus, how I thank you for my mother who valued all life. How I thank you for the white woman who valued all people, who because she believed in your word, took the risk to do what the seven churches had not been willing to do. And how I praise you that after she met my need for clothing and food and shelter, she told me about your love. I never forgot that.

> I praise you for my wife, who because of her faith, valued even me and my hurt and recognized my need for a Savior. How I thank you, Father God, Lord Jesus, that I am now a part of the Family of God, for giving me a ministry, when as a child no one thought I would ever be able to speak. Thank you for your plan for my life. And I pray, Lord God, that as we walk through this needy world, we will be touched by thy Spirit to reach out and make disciples of ALL nations. Amen.

9 – Preparing For Multi-Ethnic Ministry

– Arturo Lucero[1]

Allow me to restate a disturbing fact. For too long, the Sunday morning worship hour has been the most segregated hour in America. In recent years, fortunately, efforts have been made to change all that. There is a trend toward racial reconciliation and true brotherhood within the Body of Christ. As communities around them grow more culturally diverse, churches are opening their doors to those who do not share their language and customs.

These efforts are well intentioned and represent a definite step in the right direction. However, they often result in disappointment, division, and resentment. Too often, congregations wind up worse off than they were before they started the cooperative

---

[1] Rev. Arturo Lucero is on staff at Hesperia Community Church. He is the General Director of Bible Church Mission, the church extension agency of the Independent Fundamental Churches of America, under whose aegis thirteen Southern California churches have begun a multicultural ministry, either through Rev. Lucero's direct assistance or after participating in one of his workshops.

relationship, convinced that cross-cultural outreach simply does not work.

Multi Cultural Ministry came into existence as a result of my observations in the late seventies that (1) churches died because of the changing demographics of their community (2) and churches experienced tragic relationship breakdowns between members of the host church and a renting ethnic church.

We studied twenty-eight of the major denominations in the greater Los Angeles area to determine the impact of changing demographics on the churches and what they were doing to adjust.

The impetus for the study was the fact that many of the churches in my fellowship were dying. In the 1970s, with the growth of Asian and Hispanic communities, some churches began to rent their facilities to ethnic congregations. You could drive through parts of Los Angeles and Orange Counties and see from the portable signs written in Korean, Chinese, Spanish, or some other language that an immigrant church was also meeting in those facilities.

Yet, in spite of best intentions on both sides, they were not always happy unions. I like to compare my ministry with churches to that of a pastor counseling a young couple, madly in love, who want to spend the rest of their lives together. The pastor takes them through pre-marital counseling to help them look at some of the issues they are going to face in life. Do they have the same attitudes about finances, child rearing, how many children each desires, friends, recreation, continued education, employment desires, and things of that sort? The purpose is to help them deal with those issues before they are married so they can determine if they really want to marry each other now, later, or not at all.

After studying several churches which had allowed an immigrant church to use their facility and after talking with immigrant pastors who had been involved in those situations, we discovered that many conflicts that developed were similar to marriage relations. These churches were like young couples who married without going through counseling, thinking they knew each other. They had reasoned that they were brothers in Christ; that they each loved the Lord; and that they had common goals. What could go wrong? Only enough disappointment, division, and resentment to cause the break up of those relationships. Host congregations wound up worse off than before they extended their generous invitation to work together, convinced from a bad experience that cross-cultural outreach simply doesn't work.

Multi Cultural Ministry is committed to equipping church leaders, local church pastors, and lay leaders to transition their churches into multicultural local church ministries. We walk a church through the critical issues faced in multicultural local church ministry before they tie the knot.

Church Models. During the 1970s, there was a big debate between what kind of model to use for the structure of the church: the *homogeneous* model or the *heterogeneous* model.

The Homogeneous Model. This model describes a congregation which consists of a single people group regardless of the demographics of the community. Proponents say that the Biblical basis for the homogeneous church model is found in Matthew 28, the Great Commission. Their focus is evangelization of a particular people group. In *Bridges to God*, McGavran discusses how quickly the gospel spreads within a people group. Individuals do not want to reject their culture, their people, or their heritage in order to become a Christian. The advantage of the homogeneous principle is that the gospel generally spreads fastest through a people group when it is presented in their language and within their cultural context. When the Bible is taught in the heart language of the people, the chances for spiritual growth and maturity are increased as well.

The criticism with regard to the homogeneous principle is that adherents are accused of perpetuating segregation for the sake of numbers. The homogeneous principle flies in the face of attempts of many to break down barriers that have existed for centuries in the church as a result of segregation. Secondly, The homogeneous church model is highly susceptible to *ethnikitis*. Peter Wagner writes in *Leading Your Church to Growth,* "Ethnikitis is a disease caused by a changing community. It is the greatest killer of churches in America." Its symptom is that the people in the pew do not reflect the people in the community.

Many of you have probably heard about South Central Los Angeles, an area that erupted in the aftermath of the Rodney Green trial. Before the African American community moved into the area following World War II, South Central was a predominantly white middle class area. The established churches responded to the changing community in various ways. One GARB church gave its facilities to a Black congregation. Other churches sold their facilities. Still others dwindled down to a handful of elderly saints who refused to respond to the changing community.

As a result of the boom of the 1980s, blacks also moved out of South Central Los Angeles to the new suburbs. Then the Hispanics moved in. Now, South Central is over 60 per cent Hispanic. Black churches are now facing the same issues their white predecessors had faced. If they do not reach out to the community, if they try to stay exclusively with their same people group, their church will eventually die. That is ethnikitis.

The Heterogeneous Model. This model consists of one congregation which reflects to some degree the ethnic diversity in the community. The problem with some churches which claim to be heterogeneous is that the reflection is often token. Since there is little agreement as to the percentage of ethnic mix necessary to say that a church is heterogeneous, I will give you my definition. I define a heterogeneous church as one whose ethnic mix parallels that of its community.

The Biblical basis for the heterogeneous model is John 13:34. Here the Lord gives the second of His two mandates to the church, "A new commandment I give to you, that you love one another even as I have loved you." The focus of heterogeneous advocates is that we need to maintain unity within the Body of Christ. Since unity is so critical, they say we need to socialize and worship – not only with people who are culturally similar to us – but also with those who are culturally different. Cultural barriers must be broken down. Segregation must be eliminated. The reality of the oneness of the Body of Christ must be reflected on a local church level. That is the focus.

The advantage of the heterogeneous principle is the promotion of Christian unity. Christian unity happens among those who want it. People who attend these churches do so because that is what they desire.

Emmanuel Reformed Church in Paramount, California, is a congregation of approximately 800 that

conducts three services. It is an old Dutch Reformed
Church that is familiar with making cultural adjust-
ments to minister to those in its community. The
church transitioned from Dutch-speaking services to
English-speaking. It later transitioned from serving
only the Dutch community to serving all the English-
speaking people in its community. Pastor Ken Korver,
seeing the growing ethnic diversity of his community,
started a multiracial English-speaking service. They
utilized *The Phones for You* church planting strategy
developed by Norm Wan. An estimated 240
volunteers made 25,000 calls to the ethnics of their
community. Over 320 people who wanted to be part
of a multiracial worship service attended a new
worship service. A year later, this service averages
225. The ethnic mix is approximately 40 percent
white, 50 percent Hispanic, and 10 percent black. In
the midst of great diversity, they have a tremendous
sense of Christian unity.

The criticism of the heterogeneous principle is that
these advocates are accused of forsaking a dynamic
evangelistic outreach. In other words, they are accused of not being concerned about reaching people
for Christ. They are just concerned about having
warm fuzzies and feeling good about relating to other
believers.

The Dilemma Between Church Growth Models.
The debate over the homogeneous/heterogeneous
principle was brought to a head in the late 70s when
the Lausanne Committee for World Evangelism published a study on the homogeneous unit principle.
This was their conclusion (authored by John R. Stott):

> In our commitment to evangelism, we all under-
> stand the reasons why homogeneous churches grow
> faster than heterogeneous, or multicultural, ones.
> Some of us, however, do not agree that the rapidity

with which churches grow is the only or ... the most important Christian priority. We know that an alien culture is a barrier to faith; but we also know that segregation and strife in the church are barriers of faith. If, then, we have to choose between apparent acquiescence and segregation for the sake of numerical church growth and the struggle for reconciliation at the expense of numerical church growth we find ourselves in a painful dilemma.

These advocates have created an either/or situation. Stott continues,

We recognize that both positions can be defended in terms of obedience: obedience to Christ's commission to evangelize, on the one hand, and obedience to live in love and justice, on the other. The synthesis between these two still eludes us although we all accept our Lord's own words that it is through brotherly love and unity of Christians that the world will come to believe in Him.

I really struggled with this statement. Jesus Christ only gave the church two mandates: the Great Commission and the Great Commandment. Now, I ask you, would Jesus give the church two mandates that are mutually exclusive so that if I fulfill one I cannot fulfill the other? I do not think so. The problem is not with the mandates of Christ. The problem is with the models that man has developed to carry out those mandates.

The Hehogeneous Church Model

I submit that we need to consider a new model with regard to multicultural local church ministry. I call it the *hehogeneous* church model. It is a compound term that seeks to blend the benefits and focus of both the heterogeneous and homogeneous models. I get the "*he*" from *he*terogeneous and the "*ho*" from *ho*mogeneous. The structure of the Church must not be trapped in the miry dilemma of an *either/or* choice. It must soar on freedom's wings of a *both/and* structure.

The Nature of the Hehogeneous Model

The *hehogeneous* church is a local church whose multicultural and multilingual congregations reflect the ethnic diversity of the community.

The heterogeneous nature of this model reflects the cultural and linguistic diversity of the local church. This cultural diversity is the seedbed for the cultivation of brotherly love and Christian unity which, when seen by the world, will contribute to the fulfillment of the Lord's saying that "All men will know that you are My disciples" (John 13:35a).

The homogeneous nature of this model allows for cultural identification for ethnics which often helps them come to a saving knowledge of Christ. Donald McGavran writes in *Ethnic Realities and the Church*, "Christians … form congregations, in which they feel at home.… New converts are attracted to churches which share their cultural values." The homogeneous principle is a powerful sociological phenomenon that we cannot ignore.

The hehogeneous church is one church which consists of multiple departments to minister to the various people groups in their own cultural context and language. The Biblical bases are the Great Commission and the Great Commandment.

The Need for Such A Model

The Unity of Christ. Why do we need this kind of church? First of all, because of the high principle of the unity of Christ. Scripture teaches that we are one body in Christ and that we are to love one another.

Secondly, we need to do it to break down the we/they mentality.

When I was a young believer, I was approached by a leader of the Spanish church that rented our church facilities, "Hey, Arturo. Why aren't you over here with your own people?"

I looked at him and asked, "What are you saying?"

He continued, "Why don't you come over here and worship with us? Why are you worshipping with the gringos over there?"

That really insulted me. "Who are you to tell me who I am to worship with? Besides," I said, "I like it over here. I enjoy the teaching." That incident illustrates a major risk when a church starts an ethnic ministry. When the congregations are separate and distinct from one another, there is a tendency to compete for prospective members, particularly for those who are bilingual. When the cultural groups are organized as one church, it breaks down the we/they mentality.

I have often been asked about the integration of bilingual immigrants into the English-speaking service. Forced integration is just as bad as forced segregation, because you are forcing people to do things against their will. The homogeneous principle is a reality. It is a sociological phenomenon that you cannot deny. As a result, rather than fighting it, you need to work with it. When a church offers services in multiple languages, the believer should have the freedom in Christ to go to whichever service he or she choose. If someone happens to be bilingual and they prefer one language over another, it should not really matter. The fact is that the local church is there to minister to whatever people groups it is able to relate to linguistically and culturally. Christians need to be given their freedom in Christ to attend the worship service of their choice.

The Lack of Available Property. As director of church planting for the Independent Fundamental Churches of America in Southern California, my biggest concern was finding facilities for immigrant church plants. Most of the available facilities were old run down storefronts which were over priced and ill suited for ministry. Then if we attempted to comply with city codes for public gatherings, we would have to get sprinkler systems, handicap ramps, railings, and more. We would have to spend thousands of dollars before we won soul one to Jesus Christ. We found that if the established churches in our fellowship would sponsor an ethnic church plant, it would save the mission lots of expense because we would not have to rent or refurbish facilities.

An immigrant church is going to have to choose between two things. They are either going to pay the rent, or they are going to pay the pastor. Dr. Alex Montoya has concluded from his research in immigrant church planting that an immigrant church requires two and a half times as many tithers to support a pastor than does an English-speaking church. So, the immigrant church has to decide between paying rent or paying the pastor. When a local church hosts, sponsors, or starts an ethnic ministry in their facilities, the immigrant pastor will be able to minister full time much faster than if the congregation is out there on its own.

The Need to Minister to People at all Levels of Assimilation. It is not uncommon to have various levels of English proficiency within an immigrant household. There may be grandparents who do not speak a word of English, parents who are modestly bilingual, and teenage kids who are predominantly

English speaking. By having a multicultural, multilingual church you can minister to the entire family.

One of the biggest problems that immigrant churches have is keeping their young people. Immigrant pastors say that if our kids marry a Mexican American who is not bilingual, we are going to lose our kids because they are going to go to an English-speaking service. The same is true if they marry a non-Hispanic who does not speak Spanish. By having a multicultural, multilingual church you can minister to the whole family – everyone going to the language department where they can be served best.

Becoming A Multicultural Church

How do you deal with this *hehogeneous* church? How do you put it together? I have found that a covenant is indispensable. A Covenant is a written agreement that defines the expectations and commitments the host and ethnic church make to one another. When I take a church through the process of helping them to transition into a multicultural, multilingual church, I help them to make decisions on critical issues before they implement a multicultural local church ministry.

Decide on Structure. The first thing involves how you are going to structure your church. Are you going to be one organized church – consisting of multicultural, multilingual departments whose congregants are members of the host church and share a common facility? The distinctive here is that it is one church. It is not separate independent churches sharing a facility.

Experience has taught me that not all believers are ready to allow ethnics to come into their churches as members, but they may be willing to allow a sister ethnic church to utilize their facilities. Another option, therefore, is to function as multiple organized churches sharing one facility. The Korean church would be separately incorporated, independent, self-supporting, and self-propagating. So would the Hispanic church and the English-speaking church. They simply share the same facility. The distinctive emphasis here is on independence.

A third option is to have *optionally organized churches*. For example, Lake Avenue Congregational Church, where Dr. Paul Cedar used to pastor, had a great vision to reach the many ethnics that lived in their community. They opened their doors to them, and they gave the immigrant church the option of choosing if they wanted to be members of Lake Avenue.

If they did not want to become members of Lake Avenue, then that would be great, too. Lake Avenue made it abundantly clear that they just wanted to see the ethnic congregation reach their people with the gospel of Jesus Christ. So, they opened their facilities. The distinction here is that the relationship decision is the option of the ethnic church.

Let us say that you choose to have separate churches. How are you going to work together there? Now we are going to talk about cooperation

Decide on Degree of Cooperation. Cooperation refers to the degree of partnering in ministry between two independent churches sharing a facility. Before we get into this topic, we need a basic understanding of the process of assimilation. The first generation that comes to America clings to their culture. The second generation has a tendency to flee their culture. They are embarrassed by it. Third and subsequent generations have a desire to go back to their roots, to learn about where they came from. If you understand that process, you will be able to under-stand the advantages of having a multicultural, multilingual church.

No Cooperation. If the host church is suffering from *ethnikitis* and there is minimal cooperation between it and the ethnic church, what is going to happen to that host church? It is going to die. It is like a doctor saying, "You have a terminal disease. Here is the only medicine that will cure you." If she sets the medicine on the table for you but you do not take it, you are still going to die. It does not matter that you paid for it, that you picked it up at the pharmacy and carried it in your pocket. If you do not take the medicine, you are going to die.

Similarly, where there is no cooperation, the only beneficiary is the ethnic church. They get the use of a facility. There is not a lot of benefit to the host church because that church is still going to die.

Partial Cooperation. Partial cooperation is where members of both the host church and the immigrant church, understanding the reality of assimiliation, agree to allow the English-speaking members of the ethnic church to be ministered to by the English-speaking church. Both congregations benefit. The immigrant pastor does not have to trouble himself with conducting his ministry bilingually. The host church benefits in that a bridge to the assimilated ethnics of its community is being built. For the church with *ethnikitis,* the chances of survival are greatly increased.

There is a Hispanic pastor of a Hispanic-speaking Baptist church in Whittier, California, whose own teenage kids would stay for the singing portion of the service because it was livelier. When it came time for the preaching, the entire high school youth group would leave the Spanish-speaking service and go to the English-speaking service where they could understand the Word better. They did not grow up educated in Spanish, so they did not have all the nuances of the language or the vocabulary. Consequently, they preferred to go to the English-speaking service. This kind of shared ministry is an example of partial cooperation.

Total Cooperation. Total Cooperation is where you decide to be one church, and everybody participates in all the ministries of the church. The benefit to the ethnic church of total cooperation is that they do not have to duplicate the ministry in English because it is already there. The benefit to the host church is that it provides a bridge to the assimilated ethnics of the community.

Total cooperation entails operating as one church which offers multicultural, multilingual ministries. The benefit is that it perpetuates the ministry of the local church. As an illustration, in relay races, they pass the baton. Many communities and urban centers, are in a constant state of transition. They are constantly changing socio-economically as well as in terms of the ethnicity of the people groups that come and go. One group moves in. When they move out, another group moves in.

The ethnic group is the runner. The baton is the facilities of the local church. The running of the track is the time that God gives you to minister in that community. As your people start to move out and other people groups move in, it is time to pass the baton of the facilities on to the next group. They will then run the race until God in His timing changes situations where another people group comes in and the baton is passed to them.

Whether the two congregations merge their programs depends on the leadership. We have seen some Hispanic pastors come in with a great deal of optimism. Once they got into the ministry, however, they started imposing their own barriers. For example, in one church, the Spanish-speaking pastor responded to my question regarding why his high school kids were not involved in the English-speaking youth ministry with, "I do not care for that youth ministry."

"What is wrong with it?" I asked.

He said, "They go to places that are just too expensive for our kids."

I decided to intercede on his behalf in a conversation with the English-speaking pastor, "Brother, it is great you are inviting the Hispanic group here; but their young people cannot afford the camps and the other activities."

The pastor explained, "I talked to the Hispanic pastor. I told him we have scholarships for youth who need assistance. The issue is not money, Art."

I went back, talked to the Hispanic pastor. "Brother, I was told that your youth have been offered scholarships. What's the real issue?"

He sighed heavily and said, "Pastor Lucero, I don't agree with the way they allow their youth to dress and the music they allow them to listen to. I prefer to have our youth conduct its own activities"

Preferences – everybody has them. As you recruit an immigrant pastor, select someone who has your vision and is in agreement with your philosophy of ministry.

Decide on Membership. It is extremely important to determine the membership status of ethnics relative to the host church. Are they going to be members of your church or not? This point is predetermined when you decide on structure. I know of a church where the Anglo pastor wanted to reach the Hispanics in the church's community. He contacted a Spanish-speaking congregation and asked, "Do you have a man that you could send out to help us reach the Hispanics in our community?" The new Hispanic pastor's understanding was along the lines of, *I am going to come and work with this church and whoever I lead to Christ will become members of the church*. The host pastor's understanding was the same.

The members of the church were very supportive of this new ministry – that is, until the Hispanic contingency began to outgrow the Anglo congregation. Then certain members of the congregation told the Spanish-speaking minister to take his people and go. Why? Because it was not something to which they had been totally committed. They did not want to lose control of their church. They feared that the Hispanics would take over the facility and kick them out. Their un-Christian behavior created tremendous strife in both congregations.

The ramifications of a multicultural, multilingual congregation are: (1) the ethnic group may eventually outgrow the historical group, (2) leadership responsibilities will eventually be filled by ethnics, (3) all reports will have to be translated, as will the congregational meetings, and (4) Intercultural dating and marriages are likely to occur.

Decide on Facility Use. The objective is to determine the availability of facilities and equipment for the ethnic church. We begin by creating an inventory. The pastor and I go through the church with my beginning checklist. I ask the pastor to expand that list to cover all the equipment owned by the congregation.

When the inventory is completed, I make a request,

> Pastor, I want you to go through this inventory and identify what you will offer the ethnic church. For example, may they use the audio/visual equipment? May they use the sanctuary? What classrooms may they use? May they use a portion of the bulletin boards? May they park freely in the lot, or do you want them to park someplace else?

We identify the days of the week and the hours that are available for ethnic services and other events because people can get very territorial. One pastor shared with me about a brother who had been teaching Sunday school for over twenty years. Perhaps unconsciously, this teacher felt like he owned the room where his class met. It so happened that he had done a beautiful bulletin board display some years earlier. It was so pretty they had left it up. When the Spanish church came in, they needed bulletin board space to display their notices and events. Someone took the liberty to move this antiquated display over, kind of crunch it up a little bit, so they could post their notices.

That teacher hit the ceiling. Who gave *these people* permission to come into *my* Sunday school class and start moving *my* stuff around?

Another anecdote concerns an organist who was really upset because the ethnic congregation's organist changed the stops on the organ. When the incumbent organist would play the organ, the sound would be different than usual. She lost her composure. Who gave *them* permission to do that?

In another instance, deaconesses were upset after the immigrant church used the facilities for a potluck. "They put forks where knives were supposed to go and spoons where forks were supposed to go. They put plates where glasses were supposed to go. Pastor, nothing was put back in the right place." It did not matter that the ethnics had swept, mopped, washed, and put away everything they had used. All the complainers saw was that certain things were not put in the right places.

These are some of the compelling reasons why we need to deal with the issue of facilities. I recommend that the ministry head from each department meet with their counterpart in the ethnic ministry to train them on the use and storage of equipment.

Decide on Tenure. If the immigrant church is going to be a separate entity, how long may they stay? While not intuitively obvious, living together is often made tougher when people operate with an open-ended arrangement. Even though the hospitality may have been extended from the best of motives, the host might begin to wonder after a while, *How much longer are they going to be here?* The guests may become unnecessarily anxious about how much longer the host is going to let them stay if there was never an understanding when they would be leaving.

It takes approximately five years to plant a church and attract sufficient people in sufficient numbers to become self-supporting. When I negotiate for an immigrant church plant, I always shoot for five years. When the established church prefers, I settle for a three- or four-year term, with the opportunity to negotiate an extension after two years, if needed. It is important for all parties to be able to reflect together on how things are going. When appropriate, we ask if we may extend our stay another three years. As a result of the covenants established with our host churches, I have never had to go back and haggle with the board. I just talk to the pastor, who often gives his approval over the phone. Why? Because we worked through the issues in advance.

Decide on Finances. Determine the financial commitments between the ethnic and the host church. Probably the majority of divorces in the United States happen over finances. If there is going to be a conflict, most of the time, it will be over how money is spent.

We need to clarify what the host church's expectation is for the ethnic church with regard to finances. If the ethnic ministry is a separate church, are you going to expect them to pay rent? If you are, are you going to charge them a flat rate, or are you going to take a percentage of income? What about utilities? How are you going to determine how much the utilities have increased and what the expense sharing should be? Are you going to absorb those costs? What about insurance, the use of paper for the copier, chalk in the Sunday school room, and janitorial supplies? Who is going to pay for what?

What about the host church's commitment to the ethnic church's budget? Most ethnic and non-ethnic pastors of ethnic churches must be bi-vocational. What is going to be your contribution to that ethnic church plant? Are you going to provide the pastor with a stipend? Are you going to at least buy lunch every Sunday for his family and him? Are you going to provide him a gas allowance? Are you going to put him on your missions budget? In the church's insurance plan.

The goal is to decide an actual dollar commitment or percentage of costs. You should do that in advance. If you do not, after you live together for a while, unfulfilled expectations will start to create frustrations which become points of conflict for the congregations.

Decide on Church Extension. Church extension addresses planning what to do if God blesses the combined congregations so that you outgrow the host facility. Then you have to decide if the host church stays and the ethnic church leaves. Or, does the host church say, *You know what! We are going to let you have this facility, and we are going to build ourselves a new building in another part of town?*

A third alternative is for the leadership to say, *This has worked so well here. The demographics are pretty much the same in another part of town. So let us commission those people from the ethnic church and a core group from the English-speaking department to live in that part of town to duplicate what we are doing here.* Then you create the same kind of church over there. If you decide your strategy ahead of time, it will be so much easier when the time comes to make the decision. If you do not establish mutually acceptable parameters ahead of time, then when the point comes that somebody has to leave, people will have a tendency to become very suspicious as to your reasons for asking them to leave.

The Process of Transition

Sow the Seed. This is a process of education and vision casting. I conduct it on three levels: pastor, leadership, and congregation. If the pastor gets excited about wanting to start an ethnic ministry in the church, he arranges for me to meet with the church leadership. If the leadership gets excited, then I meet with the congregation. My purpose is to share the same information at each level so that everyone is on the same page.

There are two guiding principles in my ministry to the local church. One is to create a spirit of unity. Where there is no unity, it is not going to fly. The second is to develop a covenant. I recall a certain young Hispanic seminarian. One Sunday morning before Sunday school, his pastor approached him all excited. "Tony, I finally got the Board to approve our starting a Spanish-speaking service. You are going to be the pastor and you will start services next week."

The young seminarian was taken back by the suddenness of it all but agreed to serve. He was assigned one of the elders from the church who was also Hispanic and bilingual, and they started doing visitation. The first couple of months went very well. About twenty people attended off and on.

About that time, the church board became involved. They called the Hispanic pastoral intern in and said, "We do not want you doing visitation to the Spanish-speaking community. We want you to do visitation for the English-speaking church."

So the Hispanic intern and the Hispanic elder said, "Wait a minute! If we are supposed to be involved in raising up a Spanish-speaking ministry, why can't we do visitation to the Spanish-speaking community?"

The board responded, "You were hired to do visitation and outreach for the English-speaking congregation."

"Then why did you start a Spanish ministry?"

The board said, "We did not want to; but pastor was pushing so hard. We just gave in to it. But now we see that it is not going to work."

Does that sound unbelievable? As preposterous as it sounds, I happened. I was that young Hispanic. Sometimes, well meaning, pastors push too hard. They may want something so badly that they do not take time to build unity and cooperation with their leadership and with the congregation. Further, it may not always be the pastor who pushes. It could be an influential family in the church whose child is on the mission field with a particular people group. Such members may push so hard to see something happen that the leadership acquiesces even though their heart is not in it. When problems start to rise, the first thing they say is, "I told you so. I knew this was not going to work."

Survey for Support. Multi Cultural Ministry tries, first of all, to develop a spirit of unity. We make sure that everybody is on board and that all are committed to the new venture. In that process, I tell the leadership,

> If you want me to come speak to your congrega-
> tion, there will be two things you will need to decide. The
> first decision is what approval rating you require in order
> to move ahead. If you want a 95 percent approval rating,
> that means you are willing to risk losing 5 percent of your
> congregation. If you want a 75 percent approval rating,
> you are willing to risk losing 25 percent of your congrega-
> tion. You must decide the approval rating you'll require to
> proceed with starting an ethnic ministry.

Then I ask them to assign a group of the members of the congregation to each of the leaders after I speak. They are required to conduct an informal survey to determine if there is sufficient support for starting an ethnic ministry. They may ask a question like this, "What did you think about what Art Lucero had to say about starting an ethnic church? Is that something we can do?"

They should listen to responses without giving a rebuttal. A person is either for it, or he is against it. Then when the board gets together, they develop their tally. Either they have the approval rating, or they do not. If they have the approval rating, we continue the process. If they do not, I recommend that the pastor conduct a series on the *Two Mandates of Christ* and their ramifications to a Church in an ethnically diverse community. I encourage pastors to bring in ethnic missionaries and an ethnic choir from a local church. Any activity that will expose their congregation to the growing ethnic community and its need for the Gospel will help create the vision for starting an ethnic ministry.

If the approval rating has been attained by the informal survey, we move on to the formal survey. An official letter is sent out from the church asking members to answer a few questions anonymously. The purpose of the survey is to give church members an opportunity to voice their approval, disapproval, fears, and concerns.

Covenant. After the survey has been tallied, I return to a congregational meeting to address the concerns. Normally, every concern can be dealt with in one of the five categories of the covenant: membership, facilities, finances, time, and church extension. One example may be the question of whether the host church is going to have to take care of all of the ethnic church's kids. One way the covenant could handle that challenge would be for the immigrant church to have a nursery coordinator whose assignment is to provide additional nursery workers. The specific remedy is written in the covenant. That is the best way to deal with little issues that could later torpedo the whole relationship.

Secure the Covenant. That is the actual documentation of the covenant and obtaining approval from the church leadership and the congregation so that everyone is informed and understands exactly what is going to happen. People are not so much afraid of attempting to try something new and different. What bothers them is when leadership cannot answer their questions. If leadership can say, *This is how we are going to do such and such. This is how we are going to get there. This is what is going to make it feasible and possible for us to achieve this goal*, people will feel confident in where the leadership is taking them. If you keep saying, *I do not know. I guess we will have to cross that bridge when we get there*, that will not cut it.

Closing Thoughts. Let me end with answers to a few common questions.

> ➤ **What if our church is not large enough to support an ethnic pastor on staff?**

If this is the case, take a careful inventory and offer what you can afford: a stipend, some ministry expenses, the use of an automobile, a contribution toward housing expenses, a parsonage, medical insurance, dental insurance, and/or term life insurance. Be creative. Don't limit your options to providing cash.

> ➤ **What about the issue of illegal immigrants?**

The purpose of the church is to make disciples and teach them to obey (Matt. 28:19,20). The church is not an extended arm of the Immigration and Naturalization Service. The Church is to reach out to those in need of God's love. It is the ministry of the Holy Spirit in the lives of new converts that must convict them of their illegal status. Hispanic pastors tell stories of people who have returned to their homeland in order to begin the process of legal entry into the US as a result of studying the Scriptures and yielding to the work of the Holy Spirit.

> ➤ **Does the initial church planter have to be of the same cultural heritage as the target group?**

Sheep respond to a shepherd who loves them. It does not matter the cultural or ethnic background of that shepherd. Entrenched leadership has not always been aware of this spiritual dynamic. When I was ready to go into pastoral ministry in 1983, I asked the Southern California head of our fellowship, "Can you give me the names of the churches that need pastors? I would like to send out my resume."

He hemmed and hawed and cleared his throat before he finally said, "Art, I do not think our churches are ready for a Mexican pastor." That was like throwing a bucket of ice water on me on a hot summer day.

Happily, this leader's perception of the Body was not correct. I received a call to pastor an all-Anglo congregation. Its membership was only 18 at the time, but we built it up to 150 or so. I could probably count on my fingers the Hispanics who were in that church. People just want to be loved.

> ➤ **Does the pastor have to speak Spanish?**

It is ideal if he does; but it is not necessary in the beginning. A deacon of an American Baptist Church in central California took over the clothing distribution ministry of another church in town. He wanted to make sure that every person who received clothing also received the Gospel. He invited a friend from yet another church, 25 miles away, to translate for him when he preached. Within a year's time, they had fifty adults attending a Sunday evening service.

Another example is a Hispanic church in Denver that had been planted by an Anglo. They had a congregation of almost 200 people. A couple of Hispanics from South America were saying, "We need to have a Hispanic pastor." The reason they were saying that is because they had been highly educated, seminary trained, in South America. They had been pastors themselves. The Anglo pastor could not communicate as well as they could because his Spanish language skills could not compare with theirs. These Hispanic instigators did not feel like they and the people were being fed adequately. That is why they wanted somebody of their own background. Interestingly, the other people in the church did not feel that way. It is a matter of perception. Sheep just want to be loved and taught by the shepherd.

To the preceding question and to all the aspects of ethnic ministry, the statement of Jesus seems most appropriate: We "must be about (our) father's business."

10 – What Is the Church?

They say confession is good for the soul, but bad for the reputation. Here's my confession. When I heard Dr. Ware was having a conference, I called him and said, "Doctor, this is Ken Hutcherson." I waited for a gasp and an expression of surprise when it hit him who was calling.

"Who?" he asked as he wracked his brain trying to remember who I was.

"Ken Hutcherson," I said, nonetheless undaunted. "I would like to speak at your Multicultural Ministry Conference since that lines up with what we are trying to do here at Antioch Bible Church."

He said, "Oh yes, I remember you now. By the way, I've heard some things about you which tell me you're not ready to speak at the Conference."

---

[a] Pastor Kenneth Hutcherson, former NFL football player, is senior pastor of Antioch Bible Church in Kirkland, WA. He has served as director of the Ken Hutcherson Football Camps in Seattle for 23 years, where training in football techniques and practical Biblical principles is presented to 140 high school students each year.

Being a Christian who tries to emulate Christ in my response to disappointing situations, I took it personally. As I reflected on that conversation, I concluded he meant that I was not ready to stand in front of all those well-known warriors who are ready to do what God has called them to do at all costs. Knowing the credentials and reputations of people like Dr. Perkins and Dr. Stowell, I thought maybe I wasn't smart enough. I thought it might be because I had not gone to seminary and developed a theologically trained mind. However, I really wanted to speak at the Conference. So I spent the next six months studying God's word five to eight hours a day. Then I called the Doctor back and said, "Dr. Ware, this is Ken Hutcherson." This time I did not wait for the gasp. I went right into my spiel, "I've studied many hours, and I would like to speak at the Conference."

He said, "In the last several months, son, I've heard some things about you; and you are really not ready to speak at the Conference."

Can you believe that? Disappointed again! But anyone who knows me knows I never give up. Therefore, I went to college and took some classes like hermeneutics, hamartiology, and homiletics. I did not know what those words meant, but I thought they sounded impressive. So I called him back and said, "Dr. Ware, I really would like to speak. I have taken some high-powered classes."

He said, "I've heard some things about you in the last months or so. And son, I don't want you to get your hopes up. You're really not ready."

I said, "Listen, I want to speak so badly at the Conference. I tell you what; I'll speak for free."

That's when Dr. Ware said, "Now you're ready."

There's a lesson in that story. Persistence pays off. You see, being a professional football player, I had learned how to renegotiate contracts.

It's not Over, Yet

As I prepared this chapter, I felt like I had during a game in my rookie year with the Dallas Cowboys. We were playing the Washington Redskins, and we were behind 20 points at the end of the third quarter. We knew we could still win. But then Roger Staubach got injured at the beginning of the fourth quarter and could not finish the game. The fans threw up their hands. We were 20 points behind in the fourth quarter, and we lost our star quarterback – one of the most famous men in the NFL at that time. People thought there was no hope. They started going to their cars. The game was over as far as they were concerned.

But Dallas had a couple of rookies waiting to be heard from. I was one of them. The other was a quarterback named Clint Longley. We came into the game in the fourth quarter. That's when the game got interesting. The people who left missed the best part of the game. They left because they thought it was all over except the shouting. In a similar vein, I want to let you know that the best part of this book is just beginning.

Clint Longley walked onto the field and took charge in the huddle. On the first play, he dropped back and threw a bomb to Drew Pearson for a touchdown. That and the point after added seven points to our score, leaving us down by only 13 points. The Dallas defense took the field. I came out and made an interception.

Then Longley came back and, after a series of plays, threw another bomb --another touchdown.

Now, we were down six points. The Redskins came back with a drive down to our five-yard line. But we put on a defensive stance and took the ball back.

Like a field marshal, Clint Longley marched the team down the field. He then threw a 60-yard bomb to Drew Pearson for a touchdown to tie the game as the buzzer went off. We were able to kick the field goal because the rules allow for the point after the touchdown even though the buzzer had sounded. Consequently, we won the game by one point. So many of our fans listened to the exciting end game in their cars when they could have had a seat at the game.

Similarly, when Jesus calls us off this planet, many of us are going to have to look Him in the face and answer the question, *Why did you leave the game so early?* I don't care about your getting tired – about your thinking it was over – about your not knowing the Word of God.

Reconciliation

I am thankful that God is our God – that He has given me the insight to tell you that the only way that reconciliation is going to work is for God to take those of us who need conviction and convict us and to comfort those of us who need to be comforted.

I thank the Lord for teaching me that others may be taught. I thank the Father for one of the greatest blessings in the entire world. That is to be able to help populate heaven and de-populate hell, which means no one else has to go. I thank God for His word, for that is the only thing worth hearing.

Let me begin to wrap up by asking, *What is the Church?* I studied the Scriptures for over 15 years before we started Antioch Bible Church. After 15 years of study, I concluded that we have missed something in the modern-day understanding of the New Testament. What we are missing is a proper concept of what we were meant to be. As Dr. Dixon quoted Dr. Martin Luther King, 11 o'clock on Sunday morning is still the most segregated hour in America. According to the Word of God, 11 o'clock should be the most integrated hour because Jesus said, "They will know that you are My disciples by your love for one another."

When some people talk about the church, they think about denomination. When other people are asked, *What is the church*, they want to think about color. Many people think about what they want to think about and not what God said the Church is. My next question is, *How do you spell church?* Some people seem to spell church c-h-c-h. Many people look at your sanctuary and say, "What a beautiful church!" That is only brick and mortar, however.

The church is not the Church until "u-r" in it. Now, tell me the color of that U and the color of that R. The building becomes the Church when you and I walk into it. Until then, it is just brick and mortar. The only thing on earth that is large enough to house God is the human heart. God wants our heart to be a home for his word. For too many Christians, our heart is a hotel; and checkout time is 12:30 on Sunday.

Let us turn to an example of why reconciliation is not proceeding well. Promise Keepers is a wonderful organization. I only have one problem with Promise Keepers. They did a fantastic job when they were dealing with men and their family relationships. Then they made a mistake when they defined another goal called reconciliation. Let me tell you why. Every pastor they had up there preaching was either from an all-white church or an all-black church. None of them were modeling what they were talking about. I don't have time for hypocrisy.

I went to their rallies where we talked and talked about how much we loved each other. We would give each other hugs and we would kiss one another. Then when we left, we went back to our own state of affairs – just like many of you may do when you finish this book. I ask you not to do that, however.

Some churches where I speak have so many black people in there that I have to ask for more light just so I can see the Scripture. I speak in other churches where they talk about how much we love one another. Yet it is so white in there I have to put on sunglasses to keep the reflection off the Word of God.

It is my feeling that if the Bible says something, we should be able to do it. At least we should try. If the Bible commands it, we should not care how difficult it is. If the Bible says something, we should not care if it is popular. We shouldn't worry about what others are going to think.

When we started Antioch Bible Church, everybody said, "It's just not going to work. People like to be around their own kind." Do you know that's the greatest lie in the world. If that were true, women wouldn't marry men.

Acts provides a Biblical perspective. Therefore, we need to follow it. In addition, since it is Biblical, we should line up with it.

And Saul yet breathing out threatenings and slaughter against the disciples of the Lord, went in to the high priests. (Acts 9:1)

Now let me give you some history to bring you up to Acts 9 so you can understand why Paul is breathing out threatenings and fire. What I mean is I want to go back to Adam and Eve and bring you up to date with what is happening.

When God made humankind, He made them male and female. First, it was Adam only. God put Adam to sleep. He then took a spare rib and made a prime rib. He called them Adam and Eve. And God said *I want everybody to be together. I want everyone to be the same – in terms of male and female having the same race.* That is the way God started the whole thing off. But man sinned and fell away from God. He was then evicted from the garden.

Later, Cain and Abel got into an altercation. Being brothers wasn't enough to prevent problems between them. Can you see that that is still the issue today? We read that Cain killed Abel. Note well, the first grave ever dug was for a son. Why do you think as adults many of us are going to out-live our kids?

God replaced Abel with Seth. Whereas Cain had operated out of a fleshly bag, Seth came with faith. Later God said I never had any peace with the flesh. Look at Jacob and Esau. God said, "Esau have I hated, but Jacob have I loved."

Then when man got too big for his own britches, God said, *Man thinks they can get along without me. Since they have fallen apart, I have to end the antediluvian period.* So, He brought the flood. Early humankind was preserved in three families which descended from Noah. Whether you talk about Noah's sons or whether you go all the way back to Adam and Eve, we all came from the same family.

In spite of all this, God still wanted all of us to be the same in belief of Him. And in spite of all God's love extended toward us, man still rebelled. Man began to put together a scheme that would allow them to prosper without God. Little did they realize that God would have the last word. God decided to interrupt their communication until the day he would send power from on high to empower man to deal with the ability to communicate with everyone on earth.

So He met them at the Tower of Babel. At that time, everyone spoke the same language. God said, *I will split the nation.* When they woke up one morning, one guy got ready to say *hello*, and he said, *Ola*. Another guy got ready to say *bye*, and he said *Chao*. Another tried to say *I love you* and said *Ich liebadich*. Another got ready to say *I love you* and said, *tiem*-- that's the formal. The informal in French is *amour*.

All of a sudden, they looked around and they were confused. They no longer had a common language. So, all that said *chao* got together. All that said, *ich liebadich* got together. All who said, *hello* got together; and they separated from the others they could not understand. Not until Pentecost, when the Holy Spirit brought tongues of fire so everybody could understand one another, was the earth of one language again.

God said in the book of Acts, *I brought all human-ity back together.* Now I ask you, were unknown tongues the issue or were they given to bring people in to hear the Word of God?

Tongues made everyone look and wonder what was going on. When they came to find out, they received the Word; and many were saved.

Another important incident was a healing of the physically and economically challenged man at the Gate Beautiful (Acts 3:2-10). Was healing the focus God intended? No. as before, healing was just to attract attention to bring people in to hear the Word.

Note that after that healing, 5,000 were saved. It seems that since there were no churches at the beginning of Acts, the only way to get people together was either to hold a meeting in the synagogue or to have an apostle do a great miracle, or both.

Not only did God create a miraculous speaking and a surprising healing, the third thing God did was a killing. In Acts 5, God killed Ananias and Sapphira. There were so many people saved following that event you could not count them.

Now tell me – if we're going to go along with holding up different kinds gifts, which brought in the most people? Does that mean we should kill a couple of hypocrites in the congregation every day?

All of history funnels down through the transitional book of Acts. Since God always replaces something old with something better, He replaced the Old Testament homogeneous sacrificial system with the better system of brotherly and sisterly together, sometimes referred to by the Greek word *koinonia*.

You will recall how when *God* wanted everyone to get together in the Old Testament, they would not. That was when God said, *I need to separate you.* That was like the homogeneous church of today. After God separated them, He reached inside and grabbed a Gentile by the name of Abram and made that Gentile the founder of the Jewish nation, through whom the Messiah would come.

Homogeneity Was Never God's Way

Still, the people interpreted everything through a homogeneous filter. The homogeneous belief was that if you wanted to be a believer you had to become a Jew. They taught that you were either born into being a Jew or you needed to be proselytized into the

Jewish faith. That was the only way you could be saved in the Old Testament.

However, God intervened again, *I have a better way. I am going to reverse the process of the homogeneous church and I am going to bring into being a church for all peoples so that you don't have to become a certain nationality to be a child of God.* See? That's the Biblical New Testament Church. It replaces the old way. We never made the transition with God, however. Let me prove that to you.

In what appears to be an abrupt shift, God starts moving in a different way throughout all the cities. In a radical departure from the way He had dealt with Abraham, God decided to do it a different way. He decided not to center His work around the Jewish Jerusalem church anymore. So the center of the embryonic church left Jerusalem and put down roots in the church at Antioch. Similarly, when God gets through with the Church in this day and age, He's going to move the center of the Church from America back to Jerusalem during the tribulation period.

I take exception to those who say they cannot do anything about people's prejudices because they are only one person. Do not talk to me EVER about your being only one person. Jesus plus one is always victorious. It says in the book of Acts that when Paul was saved, the whole Church rested. One man! I do not know about you, but I plan to be that one man today. If you do not believe it, come visit Antioch Bible Church and see what God is doing.

I want to apologize to white people. You have been beaten up a lot. Everybody I have heard who wants reconciliation has been white and has left the white race and moved into the black community. Where are the black people who want reconciliation who are leaving the black community and moving into the white community? If you are going to say it is right for them to do it, get off your high horse and you do it, too! One of the worst things in the world today is to be a white male. You are blamed for everything.

A lot of times whites come in and try to help. They may come in for the wrong reasons. They may come in with the wrong philosophy. They may use money the way they want to use it. At least they come. Try to get black people to move and do something. You can't even get black people to do things together. God does not have salvation on the Affirmative Action plan. Do you think that just because many black people can't read well, that God has watered down the Gospel – that you don't have to believe the whole Gospel? Since people can't read, the only thing you need to believe is just one part of it? Is that true? Emphatically, no! God doesn't judge on a curve. Either you are either righteous or you are not.

Whites and blacks aren't the only ones who should apologize for non-reconciliation. In fact, Hispanics, Asians, and every other group needs to apologize as well. If we are the Church, we are the Church. Forget about racism and everything else. The world acts like the world. The world is dark and not believing. The reason the world is the way it is today has nothing to do with color – it has everything to do with the Church of God not standing up and demanding righteousness.

Do you understand why Paul was hot? I love this. Check this out.

> And as he journeyed and he came near Damascus, light shone around him [this is King James – the same Bible Jesus used to teach Joseph Smith]. And a light shone around him. It was a bright light. It knocked

Paul on the ground and blinded him.

Now it does not take a Phi Beta Kappa to figure out if someone could just throw a light on you and knock you on your knees and blind you, you ought to call him Lord. I do not know or care who you are. If you have the power of a laser before lasers are invented, you are Lord to me, Jack!

"What do you want me to do, Lord?" We spiritualize this. What if you were walking down the street and a light knocked you down? Think about it in terms that we can relate to today. (I truly believe today that most people believe the Bible because they do not know what it says. When they find out what it really says, they are not that crazy about it anymore. The reason I know that is true is because I can ask you a question, what is more important to you, your denomination or the Word of God?)

The light knocked him down. Can you imagine what the guys that were with him were thinking? *We are with the baddest man in the land. The whole church shakes just by mentioning his name.* And they see their giant knocked on the ground. Worse yet, he is also blind, looking up to somebody they do not see, pledging allegiance to someone they cannot hear. They thought it was thunder. And he was talking to it. They thought the boy had lost his mind.

God told him to go on to the city. *I have someone by the name of Ananias who is going to meet you.* I am going to tell you the worst recruiting program in the history of the church, and it works. Are you ready for it? *When Saul arose from the earth and when his eyes were opened, he saw no man, but they led him by the hand to Damascus.* Why? Because God had told him that He was going to send someone to meet him.

And Paul was three days without sight and neither did eat nor drink. And there was a certain disciple at Damascus named Ananias, and to him said the Lord in a vision, "Ananias!" And he said, "behold, I am here Lord." And the Lord said unto him, "arise and go into the street called straight and inquire in the house of Judas for one called Saul of Tarsus, for behold he prays, and he has seen in a vision a man named Ananias coming and putting his hand on him that he may receive his sight."

And Ananias said, "Lord, I do not want to go."

There are two words that do not go together – *Lord* and *no*. How can we say, *You are my Lord* (my Master), *but no, I do not want to obey you*? Just in case God was a little confused, Ananias explained to Him who Paul was.

Lord, I know you are busy, but you evidently do not know who this Paul is. This boy has been killing people! And he's been hurting some serious Christians. And the boy got the authority from the priests up there to come down here and kill lots.

God said, "Ananias."

Ananias said, "Yes Lord? But Paul has authority from the priests? Yes, Lord. He is down here on the authority from the high priest? Yes, Lord."

Now I wish, that Christians would obey their authority the way Paul had been obeying his. Why is the world more sold out to death and sin than believers are sold out to life in Christ Jesus?

Ananias, you might as well go. I have already given Paul your name. What does God have to do to you and me just to make us obedient? God already has many things He wants to give you and me and the Church if we will be obedient to His word. But He cannot give them to us because we are not righteous.

We may sound righteous. We may look righteous. We may act righteous even when we are not following the Word of God in its entirety. *Be like the fish, Ananias, be like the fish.*

"What do you mean, Lord? I do not understand."

You know ... the fish that had the coin in its mouth. I told my disciples to go fishing and whatever fish they caught to pull the money out of its mouth and go pay Caesar his due. In other words, go to work and you can make money to be obedient in all things as long as you work according to what I ask you to work in. And God says if you do not work, you do not eat. In our church, we are being sensitive. We do not want to feed people who will not work. Follow the Word of God. Can you imagine that fish having a conversation with Jesus? *Lord, I can just come to the edge of the water and spit the coin out. I do not have to get on that hook. Now if the purpose is just for them to get the money, why does it have to hurt?* No, I feel that that fish said, "Lord, you want my coin? You want me to get on the hook? You want me to die after they get the coin?" They never said they threw the fish back. But the fish submitted anyway.

Ananias, be like the fish. Obey me without asking questions if you know my word is black and white. People say, "Well we just cannot do that in our church. We cannot start a cross-cultural ministry. We do not know how."

Then let me tell you how. First, you go to your church and get with the leadership and you raise this question, "Do we want to do what the Bible says?"

They will say, "Yes."

Then say, "Somebody second the motion." Vote on it, then pose the second question: "The Bible says the church is supposed to look like the church in the book of Acts." Get somebody to second that motion, vote on it, and then implement it. I am glad God loved the world so much He did not send a committee.

God told him, "Ananias, I have blinded the boy. What more can I do for you? Anybody can beat up a blind man if he starts some stuff."

What does God have to do to you to get you to be obedient to his Church's call? What does God have to move out of your way? Who does God have to kill? I am a firm believer that God does a lot of bad things to people in church because of other people who do not have the intestinal fortitude to be obedient to God to do what needs to be done.

Then Ananias said unto the Lord, "I have heard by many, so forth and so on; but I will go."

But the Lord assured him in verse 15, "Go thy way, for he is a chosen vessel unto me." Listen to this recruiting program God is going to tell Paul.

For he is a chosen vessel unto me to bear my name before the Gentiles and the kings and the children of Israel, for I will show him how great a suffering he must suffer for my name's sake.

No More Comfort Zone

In my sanctified mind's eye and ear, I hear God saying,

I am going to call you, Paul, from the people that you love. I am going to pull you out of your comfort zone to get into someone else's comfort zone, to train them in their comfort zone to get out of their comfort zone, to go into somebody else's comfort zone to train them to get out of their comfort zone.

That is the Church! You see, the Church is not a little weakling.

I want you to check out the three things the Church is. The Church is offensive. The gates of hell will not prevail against it. We are supposed to be on the offensive. Gates are a defensive weapon. We are the ones who are supposed to be on the move. And if we are on the move, we are going to offend. God says His word is going to separate husband and wife, father and son, mother and daughter; and if you love them more than Him, you do not love Him. The Church is supposed to be offensive, not sitting around like some social club, hoping no one gets mad at us and passes a law to take away our tax-exempt status. There are many things in the Bible that are worth losing our tax-exempt status over.

I praise God, and I hope God takes it. Why? Because when God takes it away from us, we are going to have to work together. I have counted it up. If the churches in Seattle would work together and have our own bank, there would be $9.6 billion available.

We need to start pushing to get the churches to work together financially. Why? So we can do it the way God said do it and get out of our comfort zone. For some, it may be a white zone. For others, it may be a black zone, a Hispanic zone, or an Asian comfort zone. But, saints, that is not what the Church is.

While Jesus had Paul's attention, He made sure Paul understood His plan for Paul's life.

I am going to call you out of your comfort zone away from the people you love Paul, and I am going to send you to the Gentiles. I am going to send you to the dogs – the poorest of the poor. That is how Gentiles were looked at by the Jews. I want them in the church, too. Then I am going to send you to the richest of the rich. They need to be in the church, too. I am going to send you to the religious people; they need to be in the church.

It was the religious people Christ had the most trouble with. It was not the Gentiles who mainly crucified Christ; it was the religious people of God.

Offensive and Uncomfortable Church

The Church is not only offensive. The Church is also supposed to be uncomfortable. If we are calling people to righteousness, many of them are not going to like us. They hated Christ, so they are not going to like us. Why do we want the Church to be so comfortable? It was not comfortable in the New Testament. Everywhere they went, somebody was trying to kill them. When Paul went to a new town, he seemed to ask, "What kind of jails do you have here?" He did not ask what kind of hotels do you have here?

Not only is the Church offensive and uncomfortable, but most importantly – when God enters, the Church is unstoppable. They cannot stop us. Walls fall before the advancing church. The gates of hell fall when there are righteous people walking with the Word of God. The evildoers cannot hang with us.

Not only am I going to call you out of this Paul, but you are going to suffer for doing what you do not want to do – for leaving the people you love to go to people who are not going to like you. That is the Church. If I want to know how a Dodge truck works – I go over to a Dodge dealer. If I want to know how a Maytag dishwasher works, I would go find a Maytag man. You go to the manufacturer when you want to know how something works. And when you want to know how the Church works, go to the one who started churches all over Asia Minor and into Europe after being sent out from the believers at Antioch.

If you want to know what the Church looks like, look who sent Paul out. Chapter 13 describes this model church. When God stopped the sacrificial system, he started the Church. When He started the Church, Antioch quickly became the model. God said every church should look like this model, because every person who was in the Old Testament had to go through the sacrificial system whether they liked it or not. God said, *I am replacing the sacrificial system with the Lamb of God. Now in grace, I call all people back together from the awful rending that took place at the Tower of Babel when mankind attempted to defy me. Now the Church reflects everybody.*

Do not think that we are working together just because I let another ethnic group use our building at 3 o'clock, when my all-black or all-white group meets at 11 o'clock! Do not hide behind the façade of a contemporary service at 8 a.m., a real *jammin'* service at 11 o'clock, a real old-fashioned service for the gray-heads at 9:30. It would be a shame to even think, "Boy are we working together." You are allowing your people to stay in their comfort zone. How are the young people going to see how the gray-headed people worship if we have different services for them? Do not try to make yourself feel good on your interpretation of the Scripture.

Acts 13:1 reads, "There were in the church there at Antioch"--that is how we got our name Antioch Bible Church, because we were going to be the kind of church that was going to go back and do it the way the Bible said do it. God sent me to an all-white upper middle-class neighborhood, with lots of money – the high-rent district – to start a cross-cultural church. People said, "Ain't no black people over there."

I said, " I know there are a lot of black people over here because I see too many people on the bridge going to downtown churches from here on Sunday morning." And if we can do it in Bellevue, the high-rent district, what they call the "white vanilla suburbs," everybody else has a downhill battle.

Pastor, we would like a cross-cultural ministry, but we are rural, and there are no black people around here. Oh, really. Now God said cross-cultural, He did not say black and white. Who do you have working in your fields, out there in that pea patch and the watermelon patch and out there in the cornfields? You have all kinds of immigrants, but you are afraid for them to come to your church because they may start looking at your daughter! Everybody knows that the whole history of the church has been that the white man and the black woman have been free to cohabit. If you think I am kidding, look how many different colors we have. And it did not come from black men and white women.

"Now there were in the church at Antioch certain prophets and teachers." In addition to Barnabas, there were some Jews, some traditionalists, and then who else? There was Simeon, they called him Niger. Oh, there were some Nigers in the church too, isn't that something? Some commentaries say they called him Simeon the Black because his hair was black. I think it is the same Simon who put the cross on his back and carried it when Jesus was on the way to Golgotha. If anybody can become a believer, this man became a believer. And he is no doubt the same one who went up to Antioch to start something new. By the way, Simeon was a leader in the church because he is listed right after Barnabas. Who else was a leader? There was Lucius of Cyrene, a brother who was brought out of a whole different culture, a whole different country. And then there was Manaen. He was rich. He was from the house of Herod.

So we have in the Church blacks, whites, Asians, you name it. Rich and poor were in the church at Antioch worshiping together. That is the model that Paul was sent from, from the very beginning of the first missionary journey, the second missionary journey, and the third missionary journey to start churches that reflect what it looked like at Antioch. Then it moved to Ephesus. Now this movement has spread all over the world. And God said I am going to call this Church out at the rapture, and I am going to go back to deal with the Jews because they still reject me, but I am not through with them yet. Isn't it amazing that once we got the church moving to pray for all people, all of a sudden we say we do not like it that way. We would rather be with our own kind. Forget what God said. If the Jews did not have the right to change the model of the sacrificial system in the Old Testament, who gives us the right to change the model of the Church in the New Testament?

As we peek through the church window at Antioch, who do we see? Barnabas, a Jew from Cyprus. We Paul, a former Pharisee and church persecutor. Simeon a man from north Africa, one of the church leaders. We see Romans. We see other Gentiles

God painted the church at Antioch with a full palette. What we see is a dynamic blend of cultures and races – and the place was exploding with life! But most churches in our country today do not have that kind of color scheme or blend of cultures. We have gone backward. We have gone back to homogene-ous, one-race, one-nationality, one-culture churches. We have become "comfortable" with that arrange-ment; but it is not what God intended, and I do not believe the Lord of the church is pleased. We can please God by recovering the Antioch vision.